MARY LINCOLN

Mary Lincoln

WIFE AND WIDOW

BY

Carl Sandburg

APPLEWOOD BOOKS
BEDFORD, MASSACHUSETTS

Mary Lincoln, Wife and Widow was first published in 1932 by Harcourt, Brace and Company.

ISBN 1-55709-248-6

Thank you for purchasing an Applewood book. Applewood reprints America's lively classics — books from the past that are still of interest to modern readers. For a free copy of our current catalog, write to: Applewood Books, P.O. Box 365, Bedford, MA 01730.

10 9 8 7 6 5 4 3 2

COVER: Francis Bicknell Carpenter portrait of Mary Lincoln. Circa 1865. Courtesy of the Illinois State Historical Library.

LIBRARY OF CONGRESS CATALOGING-IN-PUBLICATION DATA:
Sandburg, Carl, 1878-1967.
　　Mary Lincoln, wife and widow / by Carl Sandburg.
　　　　p.　　cm.
　　Originally published: New York: Harcourt, Brace, 1932.
　　ISBN 1-55709-248-6
　　1. Lincoln, Mary Todd, 1818-1882.　　2. Presidents' spouses—United States—Biography.　　I. Title.
E457.25.S262　　1995
973.7'092–dc20　　　　　　　　　　94-43071
[B]　　　　　　　　　　　　　　　CIP

Acknowledgments and Sources

Three letters written by Mary Todd before she was married, the earliest known letters written by her, and not hitherto published, are used in this work. These were a loan from Oliver R. Barrett of Chicago. Mrs. Annie Bryan of Peoria, Illinois, gave the use of other letters which help interpret the Mary Todd letters and give sidelights on the relationships of Abraham Lincoln, Mary Todd, and their gossiping friends.

OLIVER R. BARRETT gave the use of many original and unpublished letters, much documentary and pictorial material, besides giving time and keen, helpful criticism. It is many years now since Dr. William E. Barton instigated a search into forgotten corners of the Probate Court files of Cook County. Judge Henry Horner of that court personally conducted this search which brought to light the dusty and never published records of the testimony and the jury verdict regarding the insanity of Mrs. Lincoln. M. Llewellyn Raney, librarian of the University of Chicago, assisted in the delving for material in the late Dr. William E. Barton's Library of Lincolniana, now at the University of Chicago.

ACKNOWLEDGMENTS

Files of Springfield newspapers in the Illinois State Historical Library have been consulted besides files of newspapers and periodicals in Chicago and New York, and numerous scrap-books in various libraries and collections. The letters and manuscripts of Charles Sumner in the Harvard University Library have been consulted. References to Mrs. Lincoln in many Civil War letters and diaries were of service; the diary of Orville Hickman Browning, published by the Illinois State Historical Society, one of the most frequent visitors at the Lincoln home who was socially approved of by Mrs. Lincoln, was of extraordinary value. For one graphic scene in which Mrs. Lincoln violently upbraided her husband in the presence of Richard M. Oglesby the evidence rests on the personal statement of a friend of Oglesby, a responsible Illinois citizen now living; his reminiscences bearing on the Lincoln family are yet to be published. Scores of personality sketches of Mrs. Lincoln in magazine and newspaper articles were scrutinized. A dozen or more books on the wives of presidents or on social life in Washington, were consulted, the most notable of these proving to be Mary Clemmer Ames's "Ten Years in Washington." Other contemporaries of the Lincolns whose writings have strict value though their personal prejudices must

vi

be discounted, are Jesse Weik whose book "The Real Lincoln" contained items not used by him and William H. Herndon in their notable biography published some forty years earlier. That picturesque volume "Behind the Scenes" by the mulatto dressmaker, Elizabeth Keckley, who happened to be Mrs. Lincoln's helper and steadfast companion in her darkest hours, is not to be taken lightly as testimony. She sketches herself as well as Mrs. Lincoln in her book, is at moments lackadaisical, and again has the vivid solemnity of the negro spiritual. A chapter in Adam Badeau's "Grant in Peace" coincides in evidence with a personal statement, not as yet published, given by Oswald Garrison Villard based on conversations with his father, Henry Villard, New York *Herald* correspondent at Springfield and during the trip of Lincoln to Washington for inauguration. Among books by writers in our own time Katherine Helm's "Mary, Wife of Lincoln" and William H. Townsend's "Lincoln and His Wife's Home Town" have charm and intimacy, deliver a unique and essential quality of the Blue Grass region of Kentucky. In the writings of Ida M. Tarbell is a human approach that could not be neglected. Dr. William E. Barton's contribution in "The Women Lincoln Loved" represents long pondering over well-ascertained facts and is

ACKNOWLEDGMENTS

a living portrait. Julia Taft Bayne when a sixteen-year-old girl had playdays in the White House; her memories, gathered in the little volume "Tad Lincoln's Father," convey living moments from days long passed. The most valuable and extensive discussion and appraisal which has thus far appeared, is "Mrs. Abraham Lincoln" by Dr. William A. Evans, published at the time the manuscript of this volume was being sent to the printers. Dr. Evans is southern born, an Alabama man, whose career as a physician of high repute has lain entirely in the North. Without glossing over Mrs. Lincoln's defects, Dr. Evans assembles the known and the controverted facts, gives his own carefully reasoned conclusions representing keen personality analysis filtered through the wide charity of modern science at its best; fine human values flow from his work.

Contents

Illustrations

ILLUSTRATIONS

MARY LINCOLN

Prologue

Tragedy works in shadows, often dealing with a borderland of dark fate where neither the doctors nor the lawyers can tell just what is happening. Violence, money cares, tongues of malice, minds gone wrong, death on death—this is the stuff of tragedy.

In the year of 1882 there was a woman in Springfield, Illinois, who sat in widow's mourning dress, who sat in a room of shadows where a single candle burned. Outside the sun was shining and spring winds roamed the blue sky. For her that outside world was something else again—it was a world she had turned her back on.

Her habit now was day on day to go to this room of shadows lighted by a single candle. The doctor called it a habit by now; she had done this so often; the shadow room was part of her life. "No urging would induce her to go out into the fresh air," said the doctor.

For her the outside world was a lost world. She had seen enough of it. Her sixty-four years had covered a wide span of turmoil, bloody fighting, wild words, bitter wrangling of brothers. Of four sons born to her three were dead and to the fourth and eldest she had given her scorn, shut the door to him, and then taken him back into her arms. In the house where she sits in candlelight and shadows she had her wedding and put on a gold wedding ring inscribed "Love is eternal." From this town her husband went away—and she with him—through tumult, heavy years, anguish—and in the babel of tongues as to whether she loved her husband and was loyal to him there stood out for her one shining page of the record—where a United States senator from Massachusetts had told his colleagues: "Surely the honorable members of the Senate must be weary of casting mud on the garments of the wife of Lincoln; those same garments on which one terrible night, five years ago, gushed out the blood and brains of Abraham Lincoln. She sat beside him in the theatre, and she received that pitiful, that holy deluge on her hands and skirts, because she was the chosen companion of his heart. She loved him. I speak of that which I know. He had all her love."

The talking about her now had let down somewhat. Yet there was enough of it lingering. She would stay with her candlelight and the shadows. It was her way of adding to her words that she was weary—ready for the silence to which the boys, Taddie and Willie and Eddy, and her husband had gone.

Yet memories would come back. As a girl and a young woman she had said that some day she would be a Great Lady. This wish of her heart she had achieved. She had been the First Lady of the Land.

And yet was she sure of this? Could memory be tricking her about it? Had she really driven in an open carriage behind six milk-white horses while crowds made a pathway and flung roses at her and her husband? Had she led promenades in the White House, attended dinners, balls, cotillions where the Cabinet, members of Congress, and the foreign diplomatic corps paid attention to the wife of the President? Had it actually happened?

No, her memory was not tricking her. She had a store room of evidence, piled high with trunks, boxes, cases. These had been brought in by cart-loads until, said the doctor, "It was really feared that the floor of the store room would give way."

Here was a roomful of apparel: gowns of silk, rich and sweeping crinolines, shawls of rare lace, hats, gloves, shoes, ribbons, personal decorations that had pleased her; each in its time was vouched for as the most modish of the moment.

5

She lifts trunk covers and takes out garments, costly fabrics, handles them, lets her eyes rove over them, gathers the feel of them once more.

Though she now wears widow's mourning garb she had in her day been set in brilliance. Her dress for the 1865 inaugural of her husband brought a bill of $2,000 from a New York merchant. She had been lavish as to gloves, one dealer in Washington sending a bill for 300 pairs which she had purchased across four months. Then there was the tin box of jewels, valued at $5,000 in court proceedings. Her keepsakes of the bygone days were a resource to her now. What was said of these mementoes—that certain of them were stolen— they were saying it in the outside world from which she was now gone. The sun world was no longer hers. She lived in the candlelight and shadow.

Even though it had become an issue in a senatorial committee as to whether she had pilfered traditional belongings of the White House—wasn't that all of the past? Wasn't it over and done with? Was she not ready to move out into the final shadows? Who should care?

It was the closing year, the end of a woman whose life since maturity seldom had a pleasure not mixed with pain and fear. The headaches, the hot tongue lashings, the babblings and accusations—it was good-by to them all and—the summer of that year—good-by, proud world!

"Her memory remained singularly good up to the very close of her life," said the good doctor, Thomas W. Dresser. "She was bright and sparkling in conversation. Her face was animated and pleasing; and to me she was always an interesting woman; and while the whole world was finding fault with her temper and disposition, it was clear to me that the trouble was really a cerebral disease." He performed a post-mortem examination. The evidence was there in his opinion that she was a racked and driven woman—that her sudden tempests and her troublesome vagaries were written in the tissues of the brain early in her life, perhaps before she was born.

So all the babblings about her are only a vain exercise of the tongues of those who misunderstand. One may go to the facts. One may say this or that happened. On such a day she did so and so. The epithets, however, all the names people called her, can be written off, forgotten. They don't count. She lived, suffered, laughed, wept, sat in candlelight and shadows, and passed out from the light of the living sun.

They carried a burial casket out over the threshold her feet touched as a bride—and that was all.

Baby Days

DAVID TODD of Providence Township, Montgomery County, Pennsylvania, was Scotch Irish, of the Covenanters who made bloody war against the Established Church of England, fled to Ireland and emigrated to America.

In 1773 this David Todd sold his land in Pennsylvania for $12,000 and moved to Kentucky so as to be nearer the homes of his three sons.

These three, John, Levi and Robert, after educations at the Virginia school of their uncle, Reverend John Todd, had taken to the Wilderness Road and gone to Kentucky.

Among the first settlers of Lexington, the blue grass town which became a university seat and a center of culture, was Levi Todd. He took a hand in the fighting that was necessary for white people to hold the new country against the red men who once owned it and for long had fought wars among each other for the hunting and fishing rights.

Lieut. Levi Todd marched under General George Rogers Clark in campaigns to hold the West against Indian tribes and British troops. When Daniel Boone gave over command of the Kentucky state militia the office was assumed by Levi Todd ranking as Major-General. His uncle, Reverend John Todd, got from the

Kentucky legislature the charter for Transylvania Seminary, later a university of which General Levi Todd was a trustee. On the Richmond Pike near Lexington and neighbor to Henry Clay's home was the large and elegant country estate of Levi Todd, named "Ellerslie."

The seventh of Levi Todd's eleven children, born in 1791, was Robert Smith Todd, who at fourteen entered Transylvania University, studied mathematics, Latin, astronomy, logic, Greek, history, and according to the university president, James Blythe, "conducted himself in a becoming and praiseworthy manner." Leaving the university he studied law and was admitted to the bar in 1811. The twenty-year-old lawyer didn't begin practice; he held on to his job in the Fayette Circuit Court clerk's office. And he paid attentions to a seventeen-year-old girl, Eliza Parker. She was the daughter of Major Robert Parker, a Revolutionary War officer, and a first cousin of Levi Todd. The Parker home, it was said, was the first brick residence in Lexington. When Eliza's father died in 1800, the *Kentucky Gazette* noted him as "an early adventurer to Kentucky—of extensive acquaintance—and universally esteemed." His will leaving farms, slaves, town lots and personal property to his widow, enjoined, "It is my sincere will and desire that all my children shall be carefully brought up and well educated."

Then came the War of 1812. Robert S. Todd, as captain of a company of raw militiamen, disbanded his men and enlisted with them in the Lexington Light Infantry. Early in the field service Todd went down with pneumonia, was brought back to Lexington, recovered his health, and decided again to go to the fields of battle. Young Eliza Parker was willing he should go. She was also willing to marry him before he should go. On November 26, 1812, they were married. On the next day he kissed her good-by and with a brother rode off to join Kentucky soldiers camped in sleet and snow on the Maumee River. They marched to Fort Defiance through snow drifts and across icy streams. They marched with an expedition against Frenchtown on the River Raisin and in a battle with Proctor and his Indians the rifles and tomahawks of the red men killed half of the boys of the company from Lexington. The *Kentucky Gazette* noted with the news, "Never have the people of this town and its neighborhood met with a stroke so afflicting as that produced by the late battle of Raisin . . . We have all lost a relation or friend." Two of the Todd brothers, Sam and John, were wounded and taken prisoner. John ran the gauntlet and made an escape; Sam was adopted into a tribe and lived with the copper faces for a year, when his liberty was bought for a barrel of whiskey. Robert S. Todd was in the thick of the fighting, came through alive, and before the end of 1813 was at home in Lexington housekeeping with the young cousin he had married.

The couple were opposites in temperament. It was recorded of them, "Eliza was a sprightly, attractive girl, with a placid, sunny disposition, in sharp contrast to her impetuous, high-strung, sensitive cousin, Robert S. Todd."

A properous grocer, a partner in Smith & Todd's "Extensive Grocery Establishment," Clerk of the Kentucky House of Representatives, member of the Fayette County Court, and still later president of the Lexington Branch Bank of Kentucky, also a cotton manufacturer, Robert S. Todd was a solid and leading citizen. The growing family that came was served by negro slaves: Jane Saunders, the housekeeper; Chaney, the cook; Nelson, the body servant and coachman; old "Mammy Sally" and young Judy, who took care of the little ones.

Two daughters, Elizabeth and Frances, were born, then a son, Levi, then on December 13, 1818, Mary Ann Todd. Like the others Mary seemed to be one of the well born. If she was a cripple at birth no one knew it. If in the soft folds and convolutions underneath the bone frames of her head there was a disorder of structure and function marked for pitiless progressions, no one saw it or spoke of it. No one could. She was born as one more beautiful baby in the world, flawless and full of promise.

A baby brother came, died in his second summer. Then a girl who was named Ann Maria and thereafter Mary Ann dropped the Ann from her name, except in signing certain legal documents.

Another baby brother came. And the house was dark. And the one-horse gigs of doctors stood in front of the house. And the children were taken next door to their grandmother.

It was the Fourth of July; artillery cadets firing cannon; church bells ringing; famous generals visiting Henry Clay at a barbecue dinner, toasts to Washington, the Union and "The Ladies of the Western Country— the rose is not less lovely, nor its fragrance less delightful because it blooms in the Wilderness."

And the one-horse gigs of the doctors waited in front of the home of Robert S. Todd. The new child, the baby brother, came. But Eliza Parker Todd didn't live through it. It was the next day that old Nelson, the black slave, hitched up the family carriage and delivered to friends of his master little cards with black borders, "funeral tickets," reading:

"Yourself and family are respectfully invited to attend the funeral of Mrs. Eliza P., Consort of Robert S. Todd, Esq., from his residence on Short Street, this Evening at four o'clock, July 6, 1825."

They buried the thirty-one-year-old wife and mother. And Robert S. Todd's younger sister, Ann Maria, came to help take care of the six children.

Seven months later Robert S. Todd had plans under way to marry Miss Elizabeth ("Betsy") Humphreys. She was the daughter of Dr. Alexander Humphreys of Staunton, Virginia. She had uncles distinguished in medicine and politics, and was herself mentioned as having "charm and culture." She quoted a First Family saying of the time: it takes seven generations to make a Lady. The talk of her possible marriage to Robert S. Todd was unpleasant to Mrs. Robert Parker, mother of Todd's first wife. She and others let it be known they did not approve. And on February 15, 1826, Robert S. Todd wrote to Miss Humphreys, then visiting in New Orleans, a letter which contained viewpoints, and embodied manners of address peculiar to that time.

"You have no doubt observed," he wrote to his intended wife, "with what avidity and eagerness an occasion of this kind is seized hold of for the purpose of detraction and to gratify personal feelings of ill-will and indeed how oftentimes mischief is done without any bad motive. May I be permitted to put you on your guard against persons of this description. Not that I wish to stifle fair enquiry, for I feel in the review of my past life a consciousness that such would not materially affect me in your estimation, although there are many things which I have done and said, I wish had never been done—and such I presume is the case of every one disposed to be honest with himself."

Eight months pass. They are engaged. He salutes her as "Dear Betsy," and is writing to her: "I hope you will not consider me importunate in again urging upon your consideration the subject of my last letter. I am sure if you knew my situation, you would not hesitate to comply with my wishes in fixing on a day for our marriage in this or the early part of the ensuing week."

The wedding came off at the bride's home in Frankfort, Kentucky, on November 1, 1826. The best man was John J. Crittenden, a United States senator.

By this second marriage Robert S. Todd had nine children. The first, a boy, named Robert Smith Todd, died a few days after birth. The others, three boys and five girls, grew into manhood and womanhood. Their father for nearly a quarter of a century was elected Clerk of the House of Representatives, held various public offices, conducted a bank which never failed, and in T. M. Green's volume, "Historic Families of Kentucky," was noted as "not a man of brilliant talents, but one of clear, strong mind, sound judgment, exemplary life and conduct, dignified and manly bearing, an influential and useful citizen."

The Daughter Grows Up

AND WHAT was the childhood and the growing-up of Mary Todd—having a father who was a fighter, an old-school gentleman, a lawyer, a grocer, a cotton manufacturer, a politician—having a mother such as Eliza Parker Todd but only till she was eight years old—having a stepmother in Elizabeth Humphreys Todd who was reported to be in earnest as to the theory that seven generations are required to make a Lady?

Certain it is that Mary Todd had the advantages of the well-to-do class. As a baby there was a large house with clean floors to crawl on, with wide rooms for learning to walk. Outside the house was a big yard, and next door the big yard of her grandmother, Widow Parker. Grass, bushes, flowers, tall trees, birds, were theirs for friends, with clean air and sky. Cooking, the preparation and serving of food, was considered an art among her people. Physically she had the comforts and was well nourished. She ran, played tag, climbed trees, invented mischief and was something of a tomboy, her playmate sisters said. Once on his return from New Orleans the father brought Mary and each of her sisters the stuff for new frocks, "lovely, sheer, embroidered pink muslin brought from France." Also for each one a doll that squeaked when its little stomach was pushed in. "The squeak sounded like 'Mama' and we hugged our babies," said one of the sisters. There were picnics in summer, barefoot wading in creeks, nutting parties in the fall, sleigh rides in winter, apple roastings at the chimney fireplace, a wide variety of games and sports.

She rode horseback and once raced a white pony of hers up the gravel driveway of Ashland where, it was said, Henry Clay himself came out to see her mount, a new possession. "He can dance—look!" shouted Mary, touching him with the whip—and the white pony went up on his white legs, forepaws curved in the air, with salutations to Henry Clay.

"What do you think about the pony?" she asked him, so the story goes. And he answered like a United States senator, "He seems as spirited as his present diminutive jockey. I am sure nothing in the State can outdistance him."

In their further talk Mary said, according to this tradition in the family, "Mr. Clay, my father says you will be the next President of the United States. I wish I could go to Washington and live in the White House." And Clay gave her the laughing promise, "If I am ever President I shall expect Mary Todd to be one of my first guests."

She early absorbed politics, it was said. While in short dresses with ribbons fluttering from her curly head she was allowed to come into the dining-room for dessert at her father's table, where she heard politicians of state and national reputation talk of the battles between Whigs and Democrats. "At fourteen she knew why she was a Whig and not a Democrat," it was said.

When she was ten years old General Andrew Jackson came to Lexington and troops, brass bands, horsemen, societies, gave him a grand turnout. Mary was for her Whig friend, Henry Clay, and told a Democrat she couldn't cheer for Jackson. "But," she added, having looked at Jackson, "he is not as ugly as I heard he was."

In the course of her quarrel with the Democrat, he said, "Andrew Jackson with his long face is better looking than Henry Clay and your father rolled into one." Mary declared, "We are going to snow General Jackson under and freeze his long face so that he will never smile again." After their words that day Mary and the Democrat didn't speak to each other for years. Thus her sister Emilie told it.

Until she was fourteen her schooling was in Dr. John Ward's Academy. He was strict with his pupils.

Recitations were held before breakfast. Classes assembled at five o'clock in the morning. In the winter Mary and her sister Elizabeth often walked in the dark before dawn several blocks to their school to recite their lessons, studied by candlelight the night before.

Of course, there were other lessons besides those at school. One spring morning Mary and Elizabeth ran out to the garden to have a look at a young wild turkey they heard cooing, "Peep! Peep!" The bird sound came from a thicket of honeysuckle vines over a summer house. It changed to a jay bird's rough call. And suddenly a mocking bird flew out. "The little rascal," said Elizabeth, "never tired of pretending to be some other creature, now a field lark, now a cardinal, now the gentle peep of a little turkey. We had hunted half an hour for that little turkey." Still another lesson, outside of school, came on the night a crowd of friends gathered to see the budding of a night-blooming cereus, supposed to bloom only once in a hundred years. It was a special occasion; the children were allowed to be up till midnight watching the slowly opening white petals of a strange flower.

She memorized classical poetry and recited it on so many occasions that friends joked her about it. She learned to sew, was the only one of the sisters who developed skill with the needle. So the sisters acknowledged.

She lived through the year cholera came; the house was heavy with smoke of burning tar; no fruits or vegetables could be eaten, only biscuits, eggs, boiled milk and boiled water. Coffin supplies ran out and Robert S. Todd had trunks and boxes hauled from the attic of his house for the dead.

And, of course, there were lessons in kindliness, humor, folk lore, from the negro slave, old Mammy Sally. She had imagination in telling of hell and the devil. The girls, listening, stopped their ears with their fingers. "We shivered," said Elizabeth. And once Mary's mischievous sense of humor rose and she asked about Satan's horns.

"Yes, honey," replied Mammy Sally, "ole man Satan bellers and shakes his head and sharpens up his horns on the ground, and paws up the dust with both his front feet at once." Mary inquired, "But what does he stand on when he is pawing with both feet? Has he four legs?" "No, honey, but he can stand on his tail and that makes him mo' fearsome like."

And Mary would argue that the devil's tail was black while Mammy insisted there was a Bible verse which settled the truth of the matter. "Neat but not gaudy

25

as the debil said when he painted his tail pea green."

She gave them her lore, did Mammy. She told them that the jay birds go to hell every Friday night and tell the devil all wrongdoings they have seen the week just passed. Elizabeth said Mary once sprang at a jay and chanted:

"Howdy, Mr. Jay. You are a tell-tale-tell.
You play the spy each day, then carry tales to hell."

From the windows of the Todd house on Main Street could be seen gangs of marching men, women and children—the black people—the slaves—handcuffed two by two—held by long chains that ran from the lead couple to the end—shambling on to the market, the auction block. The slave traders drove their human livestock by this route—marching them toward cotton and rice fields farther south.

Downtown at a public square, in the southwest corner, was an auction block where the children of Lexington saw men, women and children, sometimes a family, put up for sale to the highest bidder. In the opposite corner of the public square was a whipping post, a black locust log ten feet high and a foot thick, where negroes found guilty of violation of the white man's law, were flogged. One visitor wrote, "I saw this punishment inflicted on two of these wretches. Their screams soon collected a numerous crowd."

Mary's father was one of the twelve men called as a jury "to inquire into the state of mind of Caroline A. Turner," a woman of strong muscle and fierce temper, who had thrown a small negro boy from a second-story window onto a stone flagging below, bruising the backbone and crippling an arm and a leg for life. Another case much discussed in the Todd neighborhood was that of Mr. and Mrs. Maxwell, charged with "atrocious brutality" to a young female slave. Witnesses testified that Mrs. Maxwell and her son had beaten this barefooted, thinly-clad girl with a cowhide whip, lacerating the back, bruising the face, leaving scars on the nose and cheeks. Doctors found scars indicating she had been seared with a red-hot iron.

An emancipation society was formed in Lexington. A bill came before the legislature in 1828 aimed to stop importation of slaves into Kentucky. Among spokesmen for this bill were Robert J. Breckinridge and Cassius M. Clay, both personal and political friends of Robert S. Todd. Leading the opposition was Robert Wickliffe, father of two girlhood chums of Mary Todd. So it is clear that the slavery question as a human cause and a political issue was vividly alive and tangled for

Mary as she was a growing child and young woman.

One quiet night a knocking, knocking, went on somewhere outside the house. Mary was reading. The knocking kept on. She could not read while that knocking kept on. She cried out, "Mammy, what is that knocking?" The answer came in a whisper, "That might be a runaway nigger. We have a mark on the fence—I made it myself—to show that if any runaway is hungry he can get vittles right here. All of 'em knows the sign. I have fed many a one." It was a secret Mammy tried to keep—that any negro fugitive could have cornbread and bacon from her hands.

Over at Frankfort, twenty-eight miles away, was their grandmother, Mary Humphreys, owner of eight slaves. When she died her will gave freedom to all these slaves. One clause read:

"10th. I devise my negro girl, Jane, to my daughter, Elizabeth Todd, until the twenty-fifth day of December, Eighteen Hundred and Forty-two, on which said date the said Jane is to be free of all kinds of servitude and should the said Jane have any children before the day on which she is to be free, the said child or children if boys are hereby devised to the said Elizabeth Todd until they respectively attain the age of twenty-eight years, whereby they are to be free and emancipate from all manner of servitude, if girls they are hereby devised to the said Elizabeth L. Todd until they respectively attain the age of twenty-one years, when they and any increase they may have are to be free and emancipate from all manner of servitude."

She was a decisive character, this Mary Humphreys, whom Mary Todd heard much of, and visited a number of times. She read Voltaire and Volney. She took Mary and Elizabeth to a ball in Frankfort. And they witnessed their grandmother at the age of seventy-three, in a satin gown and a lace cap imported from France, lead the grand march. She had exquisitry, for a venerable woman. The girl, Mary Todd, once remarked to a sister, "If I can only be, when I am grown up, just like Grandmother Humphreys, I will be perfectly satisfied with myself."

At fourteen Mary Todd entered the boarding-school of Madame Victorie Charlotte LeClere Mentelle. The madame was a scholar, musician, dancer. Her husband, Monsieur Augustus Waldemare Mentelle, had been "Histographer" to the French king whose head was lost in the Revolution which had made the Mentelles fugitives from the Paris where they were born. Their school was advertised in the Lexington *Intelligencer:* "Mrs. Mentelle wants a few more Young Ladies as

Scholars. She has hitherto endeavored to give them a truly useful & 'Solid' English Education in all its branches. French taught if desired. Boarding, Washing & Tuition $120 per year, paid quarterly in advance. 1½ miles from Lexington on the Richmond Turnpike road."

At this place Mary Todd had four years' training. It was her home except when on Friday evening Nelson, the coachman, called for her and took her to her father's house in Lexington where she stayed till early Monday morning. She made French a special study and gave her sisters the impression that was the only language Madame Mentelle permitted on the school premises. At sixteen Mary took the leading rôle in a French play. "She was the star actress of the school," noted a sister.

The Mentelle school was entirely aristocratic in tone. The atmosphere sought by Madame and Monsieur Mentelle was that of the royal court of France where they had once had entrée and office. They lived on memories of King Louis XVI and Queen Marie Antoinette. They spoke of these two "martyrs" with tears. The American democracy meant nothing in particular to them except that it gave them refuge and a home.

They taught class, breeding, manners, from the feudal European viewpoint rather than the Jeffersonian. The purpose was to bring up ladies of charm, culture, accomplishments.

Madame Mentelle admitted she "spared no pains with the graces and manners of the young Ladies submitted to her care." The dances taught were "the latest and most fashionable Cotillions, Round & Hop Waltzes, Hornpipes, Galopades, Mohawks, Spanish, Scottish, Polish, Tyrolienne dances and the Beautiful Circassian Circle."

Mary Todd had a good time at the Mentelle school, happy days, even though much of what she practiced at learning was a useless preparation for the years to come.

"She was a merry, companionable girl with a smile for everybody," said one fellow student at the Mentelle school. "She was really the life of the school, always ready for a good time." Besides, "she was one of the brightest girls in the school, always had the highest marks and took the biggest prizes." Thus the recollection of a Louisville woman many years after.

And Mary Todd had a good time in Lexington after she left the Mentelle school. There were homes in which girls gathered, played the piano, sang songs, and learned to waltz if their parents were Episcopalians like the Todds and if they could find young men to teach them. There were lectures on week nights, and twice on Sunday services at the churches, where every one who was any one went in what the Mentelle girls called one "grande toilette." There was a public ball when the legislature came from Frankfort in a body. And there were always parties, gala occasions when supper was served at midnight and when dawn broke before heavy-eyed coachmen handed the ladies into their carriages.

Life to Mary Todd was fresh, brimming with excitement. One of her most intimate friends, Margaret Stuart Woodrow, pictured her as abundantly alive, vibrant to sensations. They rode horseback together many a time, balanced on side-saddles, wearing long plumed hats and long skirts. Said Mrs. Woodrow: "She was very highly strung, nervous, impulsive, excitable, having an emotional temperament much like an April day, sunning all over with laughter one moment, the next crying as though her heart would break."

And her sister, Elizabeth, telling of Mary and the impressions men made on her in these early Lexington days, wrote: "Among them were many scholarly, intellectual men; but Mary never at any time showed the least partiality for any one of them. Indeed, at times, her face indicated a decided lack of interest and she accepted their attention without enthusiasm. Without meaning to wound, she now and then could not restrain a witty, sarcastic speech that cut deeper than she intended, for there was no malice in her heart. She was impulsive and made no attempt to conceal her feeling; indeed, that would have been impossible, for her face was an index to every passing emotion."

William H. Townsend, a Lexington man who sought for all existing records and interviews that would testify regarding the Mary Todd who grew up in Lexington, wrote the impression: "Brilliant, vivacious, impulsive, she possessed a charming personality marred only by a transient hauteur of manner and a caustic, devastating wit that cut like the sting of a hornet."

Winding Paths to Marriage

ONE OF THE EARLIEST KNOWN PHOTOGRAPHS
OF ABRAHAM LINCOLN

(Original in the Library of Congress)

"SHE IS THE VERY CREATURE OF EXCITEMENT,"
WROTE JAMES CONKLING TO MERCY LEVERING
OF THEIR GIRL FRIEND, MARY TODD, IN 1840

Unique proof from an unfinished engraving
(In the collection of Oliver R. Barrett)

YOUNG women ready to consider marriage are not so common in a pioneer region. They are usually taken for better or worse early after arrival. And in the period in which Mary Todd came to southern Illinois, a former Kentuckian, John J. Hardin, who later defeated an important rival in a campaign for Congress, told of the scarcity of young women in an odd paragraph of a letter to a friend back in Kentucky. Hardin wrote, "Concerning the great and important matter of girls, it is not in my power to boast much. We have some sprightly ladies in town though they are few and indeed when this state is compared with yours in that respect it falls short indeed. I think it would improve if it were not for one reason, the girls get married so soon there is no time for improvement. Enterprising young men are numerous and when they have entered their land they want wives and will have them. It has occurred to me that a considerable speculation might be made by a qualified person who would bring out a cargo of the ladies. You recollect in the first settlement of Virginia a cargo of that description was brought in and sold for 150 pounds of tobacco per head. If they should be landed here shortly they might command in market at least several head of cattle apiece. Besides it would be a very great accommodation to many young ladies of my acquaintance who have been a long time trying to make an equal swap but as yet have not succeeded."

Up into this region to Springfield had come three Todd sisters. Elizabeth at fourteen was engaged to Ninian W. Edwards and at sixteen married him. Frances in 1839 had married William Wallace, a practicing physician, who kept a drug store in Springfield. And it may be that Mary Todd felt she might come across luck—or fate—where her sisters had.

When Mary Todd, twenty-one years old, came in 1839 to live with her sister, Mrs. Ninian W. Edwards [Elizabeth Todd], she was counted an addition to the social flourish of the town. They spoke in those days of "belles." And Mary was one. Her sister told how she looked. "Mary had clear blue eyes, long lashes, light brown hair with a glint of bronze, and a lovely complexion. Her figure was beautiful and no Old Master ever modeled a more perfect arm and hand." Whatever of excess there may be in this sisterly sketch it seems certain that Mary Todd had gifts, attractions, and was among those always invited to the dances and parties of the dominant social circle. Her sister's husband once remarked as to her style, audacity or wit, "Mary could make a bishop forget his prayers."

A niece of Mary Todd wrote her impression of how her aunt looked at twenty-two in the year 1840, when her eyes first lighted on Abraham Lincoln. As an impression it has its value, serving as the viewpoint and testimony of some of those who found adorable phases in Mary Todd. In this presentation she is a rare and cherished personage with "faint wild rose in her cheeks," tintings that came and went in the flow of her emotions. "Mary although not strictly beautiful, was more than pretty. She had a broad white forehead, eyebrows sharply but delicately marked, a straight nose, short upper lip and expressive mouth curling into an adorable slow coming smile that brought dimples into her cheeks and glinted in her long-lashed, blue eyes. Those eyes, shaded by their long, silky fringe, gave an impression of dewy violet shyness contradicted fascinatingly by the spirited carriage of her head. She was vital, brilliant, witty and well trained in all the social graces from earliest childhood. She could now without rebuke, wear the coveted hoop skirts of her childish desire, and with skirts frosted with lace and ruffles she ballooned and curtsied in the lovely French embroidered swisses and muslins brought up to her from New Orleans by her father. In stockings and slippers to match the color of her gown, all pink and white, she danced and swayed as lightly and gayly as a branch of fragrant apple blossoms in a gentle spring breeze. From her pink dimpled cheeks to her sophisticated pink satin slippers, she was a fascinating alluring creature." Such, in one viewpoint, was the woman Lincoln gathered in his arms some time in 1840 when they spoke pledges to marry and take each other for weal or woe through life.

For two years Mary Todd haunted Lincoln, racked him, drove him to despair and philosophy, sent him searching deep into himself as to what manner of man he was. In those two years he first became acquainted with a malady of melancholy designated as hypochondriasis, or "hypo," an affliction which so depressed him that he consulted physicians. What happened in those two years?

Some time in 1840, probably toward the end of the year, Lincoln promised to marry Miss Todd and she was pledged to take him. It was a betrothal. They were engaged to stand up and take vows at a wedding. She was to be a bride; he was to be a groom. It was explicit.

Whether a wedding date was fixed, either definitely or approximately, does not appear in Mary Todd's letter to Mercy Levering in December of 1840. Whether in that month they were engaged at all or not also fails to appear. In this letter, however, we learn of Mary Todd, her moods and ways, at that time. She writes from Springfield, giving the news to her friend, mentioning Harriet Campbell who "appears to be enjoying all the sweets of married life." She refers to another acquaintance as ready to perpetrate "the crime of matrimony." This is light humor, banter, for the surmise is offered, "I think she will be much happier."

Certain newly married couples, she observes, have lost their "silver tones."

She raises the question, "Why is it that married folks always become so serious?"

She is puzzled, perplexed, about marriage; it is one of life's gambles; there seem to be winners and losers. Her moods shift. Her head is full of many events and people that may affect her fate. She sees time plowing on working changes. She reports what the marching months have done to a prairie stream. "The icy hand of winter has set its seal upon the waters, the winds of Heaven visit the spot but roughly, the same stars shine down, yet not with the same liquid, mellow light as in the olden time, some forms and memories that enhanced the place have passed by."

Reading along in this December letter of Mary Todd one may gather an impressionistic portrait of her, a

ATTENTION!
THE
PEOPLE!!

A. LINCOLN, ESQ'R.,

OF *Sangamon County*, one of the *Electoral Candidates*, will ADDRESS the PEOPLE

This Evening!!

At Early Candlelighting, at the *OLD COURT ROOM,* (Riley's Building.)
By request of
MANY CITIZENS.
Thursday, April 9th, 1840.

HANDBILL ADVERTISING THE RISING YOUNG POLITICIAN, A. LINCOLN, AS YET UNMARRIED, TO SPEAK AT "EARLY CANDLELIGHTING" little mezzotint. She can speak with grace. "Pass my imperfections lightly as usual," she writes Mercy. "I throw myself on your amiable nature, knowing that my shortcomings will be forgiven." She is aware of her tendency to be chubby. "I still am the same ruddy *pine-knot,* only not quite so great an exuberance of flesh, as it once was my lot to contend with, although quite a sufficiency."

Mary Todd made a little forecast in this letter. "We expect a very gay winter," she wrote. "Evening before last my sister gave a most agreeable party; upwards of one hundred graced the festive scene." Matilda Edwards, a cousin of Ninian Edwards, had come on from Alton. The party was for her. "A lovelier girl I never saw," writes Mary Todd.

It wasn't so gay a winter, however, either for one or the other of the engaged couple. Lincoln was uneasy, worried. Months of campaigning, traveling in bad weather, eating poorly cooked food and sleeping in rough taverns had made his nerves jumpy. He saw reasons why marriage would not be good for him or for Mary Todd. He wrote a letter to her, begging off. Then he showed the letter to Speed, whose reputation was lively for falling in love and falling out again. Speed threw the letter into the fire, saying in effect that such feelings of the heart shouldn't be put onto paper and made a record that could be brought up later. It was New Year's Day, 1841. Lincoln went to the Edwards house and came back to Speed. He explained that he had told Mary all that was in the letter. And Mary broke into tears, Lincoln took her into his arms, kissed her, and the engagement was on again.

But Lincoln was wretched. He had yielded to tears, had sacrificed a reasoned resolve because he couldn't resist the appeal of a woman's grief. Mary Todd saw his condition, saw that he was not himself, saw further that anything between them was impossible until he should recover. And so, regretfully but without bitterness, she released him from the engagement.

Over Springfield in the circles of these two principal persons the word spread that Mary Todd had jilted Lincoln. After leading him on, encouraging him, she suddenly had decided it was not for the best. So there would be no wedding. And both were content to let the bald fact stand without explanation.

Then Lincoln broke down completely. Two weeks after the night he had tried to tell Mary Todd how he felt and had failed, he took to his bed, miserably sick. Only Speed and Doctor Henry saw him. Six days later he was up and around, due, it was said, to the strong

44

brandy which the doctor had prescribed in large quantities. But he was not the old-time Lincoln. How he looked to others was told by James C. Conkling in a letter to his fiancée, Mercy Levering, Mary Todd's close friend. "Poor Lincoln! How are the mighty fallen!" wrote Conkling. "He was confined about a week but though he now appears again he is reduced and emaciated in appearance and seems scarcely to possess strength enough to speak above a whisper. His case is at present truly deplorable but what prospect there may be for ultimate relief I cannot pretend to say." No keen or quick sympathy for Lincoln stands forth from Conkling's letter. He writes as though he and others of a limited circle were watching a man recovering from punishment received in the tangles of an ancient trap, suffering of a sort all men and women must know in the pilgrimage of life. As one of Bobby Burns's poems declares none has the right to expect sympathy for toothache, thus also there is a sort of unwritten law that those smitten with love, and rejected by the ones loved, must expect kindly laughter rather than tears from their friends. Howsoever that may be we have Conkling's letter saying of Lincoln, "I doubt not but he can declare 'That loving is a painful thrill. And not to love more painful still,' but would not like to intimate that he has experienced 'That surely 'tis the worst of pain To love and not be loved again.' "

Lincoln wrote two letters to his law partner, Congressman John T. Stuart at Washington, D. C. In one letter he notes, "I have within the last few days, been making a most discreditable exhibition of myself in the way of hypochondriasm." In the second letter: "I am now the most miserable man living. If what I feel were equally distributed to the whole human family, there would not be one cheerful face on the earth. Whether I shall ever be better I cannot tell; I awfully forbode I shall not. To remain as I am is impossible; I must die or be better, it appears to me."

His doctor, A. G. Henry, advised a change of scene, a complete break from his present surroundings. He would go to Bogota, Columbia, if Stuart could get him the consulate at that South American port. He wrote, referring to the effort Stuart was making to have him appointed consul, "The matter you spoke of on my account you may attend to as you say, unless you shall hear of my condition forbidding it. I say this because I fear I shall be unable to attend to any business here, and a change of scene might help me. If I could be myself, I would rather remain at home with Judge Logan. I can write no more."

Stuart failed to land the consulate. And Lincoln never saw the shores of South America.

In weeks and months that followed, the limited circle of insiders who believed they knew "what was going on," whispered, spoke and wrote to each other about Lincoln's being jilted by Mary Todd. "Poor A—," wrote Mercy Levering in February. "I fear his is a blighted heart! perhaps if he was as persevering as Mr. W— he might be finally successful." And Conkling replied, "And L. poor hapless swain who loved most true but was not loved again—I suppose he will now endeavor to drown his cares among the intricacies and perplexities of the law."

The memory of Lincoln, the story teller, the gay one, remained fresh, and Conkling recalled it. "No more will the merry peal of laughter ascend *high in the air,* to greet his listening and delighted ears. He used to remind me sometimes of the pictures I formerly saw of old Father Jupiter, bending down from the clouds, to see what was going on below. And as an agreeable smile of satisfaction graced the countenance of the old heathen god, as he perceived the incense rising up—so the face of L. was occasionally distorted into a grin as he succeeded in eliciting applause from some of the fair votaries by whom he was surrounded.

47

But alas! I fear his shrine will now be deserted and that he will withdraw himself from the society of us inferior mortals."

Mary Todd meantime moved gayly and serenely through the little social whirl of Springfield. "Miss Todd and her cousin, Miss Edwards," Conkling wrote to Mercy Levering, "seemed to form the grand centre of attraction. Swarms of strangers who had little else to engage their attention hovered around them, to catch a passing smile." And with what he meant to be humor of some sort Conkling added, "By the way, I do not think they were received, with even ordinary attention, if they did not obtain a broad grin or an obstreperous laugh."

A letter of Mary's written to Mercy Levering in June of the summer of 1841 shows that her heart was not so gay after all. And furthermore, she didn't believe that everything was over and the past all sealed so far as she and Lincoln were concerned.

"The last three months have been of *interminable* length," she confesses. "After my gay companions of last winter departed, I was left much to the solitude of my own thoughts, and some *lingering regrets* over the past, which time can alone overshadow with its healing balm. Thus has my *spring time* passed. Summer in all its beauty has come again. The prairie land looks as beautiful as it did in the olden time, when we strolled together and derived so much of happiness from each other's society—this is past and more than this."

Meantime also rumors traveled that Mary Todd was seriously interested in Edwin B. Webb, a widower. Mary assures her friend Mercy these rumors are mistaken. She writes in this June letter that many visitors are in Springfield for the court sessions. "But in their midst the *winning widower* is not. Rumor says he with some others will attend the supreme court next month."

Mercy Levering in her last letter to Mary Todd had intimated that Mary and the widower were "dearer to each other than friends." Now Mary proceeds to put herself on record as to this. "The idea was neither new nor strange, dear Merce. The knowing world, have coupled our names for months past, merely through the folly and belief of another, who strangely imagined we were attached to each other. In your friendly and confiding ear allow me to whisper that my *heart can never be his*. I have deeply regretted that his constant visits, attention &c should have given room for remarks, which were to me unpleasant. There being a slight difference of some eighteen or twenty summers in our years, would preclude all possibility of congeneality of feeling, without which I would never feel justifiable in resigning my happiness into the safe keeping of another, even should that other be, far too worthy for me, with his two *sweet little objections.*"

Was she at this time keeping Lincoln in mind and heart for marriage? We can only guess and surmise. It is reasonably certain that Lincoln used with Mary Todd the same words, the same point, he made with Mary Owens three years previous when he wrote Miss Owens to whom he was sort of tentatively engaged. "There is a great deal of flourishing about in carriages here, which it would be your doom to see without sharing it. You would have to be poor, without the means of hiding your poverty. Do you believe you can bear that patiently?"

Lincoln took marriage as a bargain between two persons and he wished the terms of the bargain to be crystal clear, if possible. With Mary Owens, before they went their separate ways, he had been crystal clear. And he probably spoke to Mary Todd the same sort of words he put on paper for Mary Owens. Not often does the pre-nuptial writer of love letters make himself quite so lucid as did Lincoln in writing Mary Owens: "Whatever woman may cast her lot with mine, should any ever do so, it is my intention to do all in my power to make her happy and contented; and there is nothing I can imagine that would make me more unhappy than to fail in the effort. I know I should be much happier with you than the way I am, provided I saw no signs of discontent in you. What you have said to me may have been in the way of jest, or I may have misunderstood it. If so, then let it be forgotten; if otherwise, I much wish you would think seriously before you decide. What I have said I will most positively abide by, provided you wish it. My opinion is that you had better not do it."

On this presentation Mary Owens had released him. Perhaps on the same sort of presentation on "the fatal first of January" Mary Todd had on second thought released him.

Was it possible also that Lincoln knew well it was true, as others said, and as he himself said, that he was no ladies' man, that he was, as Mary Owens declared "deficient in the little links that make for woman's happiness"? Would that explain why his words to Mary Owens in a letter, seemed rather to smack of justice than of passion and affection? Perhaps Lincoln knew that love which has not yet been tested by the stress and storm of life is a bewildering and tangled mesh to those who have their feet in it. Perhaps he was uncannily aware of, and did not care to join in with, the flaming folly of those lovers who out of wild embraces cry, "Love like ours can never die!" Perhaps he was suspicious that the fiercest loves soon burn out; he would rather have plain affection than consuming passion. Possibly he saw eye to eye with Henrik Ibsen declaring, "There is no word that has been soiled with lies like that word love."

Something like this was in his heart and head when he wrote Mary Owens words of a sort that he may have repeated to Mary Todd. "You must know that I cannot see you or think of you with entire indifference; and yet it may be that you are mistaken in regard to what my real feelings toward you are. If I knew you were not, I should not trouble you with this letter. Perhaps any other man would know enough without further information; but I consider it my peculiar right to plead ignorance, and your bounden duty to allow the plea. I want in all cases to do right, and most particularly so in all cases with women. I want at this particular time, more than anything else, to do right with you; and if I knew it would be doing right, as I rather suspect it would, to let you alone, I would do it."

Something like this, in viewpoint and theory as to relationships between man and woman before mar-

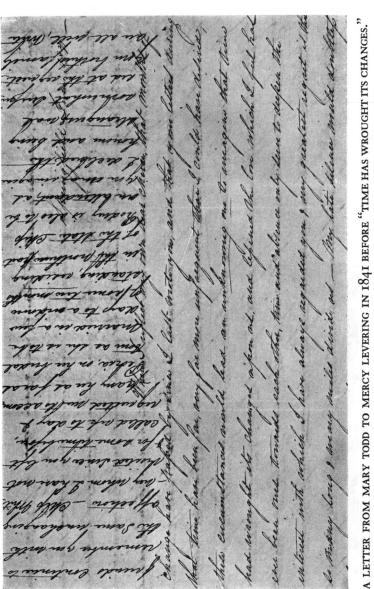

A LETTER FROM MARY TODD TO MERCY LEVERING IN 1841 BEFORE "TIME HAS WROUGHT ITS CHANGES." IN AN ECONOMICAL POSTSCRIPT SHE WRITES OF HER REFUSAL TO ACCOMPANY A FRIEND ON HER BRIDAL TOUR "AS FAR AS PEORIA"

MARY LINCOLN
GOWNED IN A DOLLY
VARDEN PATTERN
OF THE
VICTORIAN PERIOD

riage, may have been in his heart and head when he spoke with Mary Todd. Farther back would be viewpoints of life and the laughing philosopher's contemplations involved in Lincoln's Rabelaisian letter to Mrs. Orville H. Browning on how and why Mary Owens released him from their tentative engagement.

And now though Mary Todd had sent him a letter releasing him from their engagement, Mary in her June letter of 1841 to Mercy Levering is referring to Joshua Speed, Lincoln's friend and roommate. She has had a letter from Speed who is visiting his old home in Kentucky. Speed brings to mind Lincoln and she writes of him. "*His* worthy friend [Lincoln], deems me unworthy of notice, as I have not met *him* in the gay world for months. With the usual comfort of misery, [I] imagine that others were as seldom gladdened by his presence as my humble self, yet I would that the case were different, that he would once more resume his station in Society, that 'Richard should be himself again.' Much, much happiness would it afford me."

The implication was there in her letter that time would bring her and Lincoln together again. Though she had been in the social whirl, danced with other men, had her name linked with suitors for marriage, Lincoln was talked of as solitary. Her hope was, so she wrote Mercy Levering, that "Richard should be himself again," that Lincoln would recover from the bad health, the nervous exhaustion, which marked him in the winter of 1840.

Now that his roommate, Speed, had gone to Kentucky, Lincoln began rooming at the house where he had boarded, taking his meals, since coming to Springfield. There also had lived Sarah Rickard, dark-haired and seventeen, disconsolate at the departure of Speed of the "ever-changing heart." Lincoln and Sarah went places together. They saw a melodrama, "Babes in the Wood," wherein the babes died in the forest and little birds came and covered them over with leaves. Once Lincoln joked of marriage. There was Biblical precedent for a union between Sarah and Abraham, he said with raillery in his voice and eyes. Sarah moved into the country, and there, at intervals, Lincoln visited her, reporting the state of her feelings to his friend in Kentucky. Under his ministrations the girl forgot the hurt that had been in her heart since Speed had gone, so that Lincoln wrote to him: "One thing I can tell you which I know you will be glad to hear, and that is that I have seen Sarah and scrutinized her feelings as well as I could, and am fully convinced she is far happier now than she has been for the last fifteen months past."

And of these things biographers, innocently misled by the mysterious deletion of a name in letters and by statements not quite frank from elderly men and women, have made a tale of Lincoln and a love he never felt.[1]

Early in 1841 Speed sold his store in Springfield and went to Kentucky. In August Lincoln went to visit him, to rest for weeks in the big Speed home near Louisville. There he met Fanny Henning, the young woman Speed was planning to marry. The wedding date was set. Lincoln went back to Springfield but for months he and Speed were haunted by the approaching wedding. Speed was as shaken and worried about it as Lincoln had been about his affair with Mary Todd. Speed returned to Springfield for a long visit but on leaving for Kentucky again Lincoln handed him a letter to read on the stage to St. Louis and the steamboat for Louisville. The letter was an argument fortifying Speed and giving him reasons and courage for going through with his wedding as planned. "I know what the painful point is with you at all times when you are unhappy: it is an apprehension that you do not love her as you should. What nonsense!"

[1] A more detailed presentation of the Sarah Rickard episode is on page 344.

Speed reached home, found his intended bride sick, the doctors worried. He wrote Lincoln he was in the depths of misery. Lincoln replied, "Why, Speed, if you did not love her, although you might not wish her death, you would most certainly be resigned to it." He asked pardon if he was getting too familiar. "You know the hell I have suffered on that point, and how tender I am upon it."

Speed married Fanny Henning in February of 1842, and Lincoln's letter of congratulation declared, "I tell you, Speed, our forebodings (for which you and I are peculiar) are all the worst sort of nonsense." Speed had written that something indescribably horrible and alarming still haunted him. He implied marriage was no good to him. Lincoln predicted, "You will not say *that* three months from now, I will venture. When your nerves get steady now, the whole trouble will be over forever. Nor should you become impatient at their being very slow in becoming steady." Thus the recovering victim of "nerves" assured one struggling.

Also in this advice to Speed Lincoln includes a little argument that both he and Speed had been dreaming fool dreams about marriage bringing an impossible paradise. They had overrated the benefits and romance of matrimony. "You say, you much fear that the

Elysium of which you and I dreamed so much is never to be realized. Well, if it shall not, I dare swear it will not be the fault of her who is now your wife. I now have no doubt, that it is the peculiar misfortune of both you and me to dream dreams of Elysium far exceeding all that anything earthly can realize."

When, a month later, Speed wrote that he was happy and Lincoln's predictions had come true, Lincoln replied, "Your last letter gave me more pleasure than the sum total of all I have enjoyed since that fatal first of January, 1841." Again he refers to Mary Todd. She still haunts him. "Since then it seems to me that I should have been entirely happy, but for the never absent idea that there is *one* still unhappy whom I have contributed to make so. That still kills my soul. I cannot but reproach myself for even wishing to be happy while she is otherwise. She accompanied a large party on the railroad cars to Jacksonville last Monday, and on her return spoke, so that I heard of it, of having enjoyed the trip exceedingly. God be praised for that!"

Speed now sent a warning that Lincoln must either soon make up his mind to marry Miss Todd or put her out of his thoughts completely, forget her. This was correct advice, Lincoln wrote back. "But, before I resolve to do one thing or the other, I must gain my confidence in my own ability to keep my resolves when they are made. In that ability, you know I once prided myself, as the only or chief gem of my character; that gem I lost, how and where you know too well. I have not yet regained it; and, until I do, I cannot trust myself in any matter of much importance."

Perhaps Lincoln used some of these very words to Mary Todd when later in 1842 they were brought together at the home of Mrs. Simeon Francis, wife of Lincoln's friend, the editor of the Sangamo *Journal*. Neither Lincoln nor Mary Todd knew beforehand they were to be brought face to face by Mrs. Francis, so it was said. It was a pleasant surprise. The first meeting was followed by many others. Among the very few who knew of these meetings was Julia Jayne, a close friend of Mary Todd. With these two young women Lincoln joined in the fall of 1842 in writing pieces for the Sangamo *Journal* satirizing James Shields, state auditor, who challenged Lincoln to a duel which at the finish dissolved into apologies that meant nothing in particular. Yet it was an adventure with fresh excitements daily; it drew the couple closer.

Early in October Lincoln wrote Speed he knew well that Speed was happier than when first married. He could see in Speed's letters "the returning elasticity of spirits" resulting from marriage. "But," he wrote, "I want to ask you a close question. 'Are you now in *feeling*, as well as *judgment*, glad you are married as

PAGE HEADED "FAMILY RECORD" IN THE LINCOLN FAMILY BIBLE. THE FIRST ENTRY IS IN THE HANDWRITING OF ABRAHAM LINCOLN; THE SECOND IN THAT OF ROBERT TODD LINCOLN

you are?' From anybody but me this would be an impudent question, not to be tolerated; but I know you will pardon it in me. Please answer it quickly, as I am impatient to know."

Speed's answer to Lincoln, it seemed, was yes, he was

glad both in feeling and judgment that he had married as he did.

A few weeks later, on November 4, 1842, Lincoln and Mary Todd were married at the Ninian W. Edwards home. The Reverend Charles Dresser in canonical robes performed the ring ceremony for the groom, thirty-three years old, and the bride, twenty-three years old.

Mary Todd was now to have fresh light on why newly married couples lose their "silver tones," if they do. She was to know more clearly the reply to her query of two years previous, "Why is it that married folks always become so serious?"

In one of his letters advising Speed to marry, Lincoln had written that his old father used to say, "If you make a bad bargain, hug it all the tighter."

In a letter five days after his wedding to a Shawneetown lawyer regarding two law cases, Lincoln closed with writing, "Nothing new here, except my marrying, which, to me, is a matter of profound wonder."

Twenty-four years later Joshua Speed wrote Herndon, "If I had not been married and happy—far more happy than I ever expected to be—Lincoln would not have married."

Twenty-two Years of Marriage

THIS was the beginning of the twenty-two years of married life for this oddly-matched couple. They were "the long and the short of it," as Lincoln said more than once. The wife was sensitive about the picture they made standing alongside each other; she never allowed a photograph to be made of them as a couple. They were opposites in more than height. She was chubby; he was lean. She was swift of tongue and vehement in phrase; he was reserved and drawling. While he was rated as coming from the lower working class, "scrubs," she considered herself as indubitably of the well-bred upper class, patrician, and according to one of her sisters, she was in a vexed mood for a moment on the night of her wedding and made a reference to the difficulties in being involved with "plebeians."

The contrast between them which grew in the years was in temper or control. She grew more explosive; her outbursts came at more frequent intervals, were more desperate exhibitions, enacted in the presence of more important persons. Her physical resources and mental ability took on such added pathos from year to year that in a wide variety of ways many who met her referred to her as "a sad case." This while her husband's patience developed, his self-discipline deepened, and in the matter of self-control, knowing what he was doing while he was doing it, he was increasingly noted as a marvel.

The houses they lived in marked their pilgrimage together, (1) the Globe Tavern in Springfield where they lived cheaply and made plans, (2) the one-and-a-half story Eighth Street house where they set up housekeeping, (3) Mrs. Spriggs' modest boarding house in Washington, D. C., (4) the Eighth Street house in Springfield with a full second story added, (5) the White House in Washington, D. C., also known as the Executive Mansion.

Nearly always between these two there was a moving undertow of their mutual ambitions. Though his hope of achievement and performance was sometimes smothered and obliterated in melancholy, it was there, burning and questing, most of the time. And with Mary Todd Lincoln the deep desire for high place, eminence, distinction, seemed never to leave her. And between these mutual ambitions of theirs might be the difference that while he cared much for what History would say of him, her anxiety was occupied with what Society, the approved social leaders of the upper classes, would let her have.

As a newly elected Congressman's wife in 1846, she

had gay pulses; she had predicted her husband would go up the ladder and she with him. On his trip to Washington to sit in Congress, she took him by a detour to Lexington, Kentucky, to meet her relatives and the playmates of her youth. She joined him later in Washington where they lived at the plain boarding house of Mrs. Spriggs—and where he saved enough of his salary to pay off the last of the store-keeping debts he got loaded with about twelve years earlier when he learned that as a merchant he was a total loss.

Then her gay pulses as a Congressman's wife went down as her husband lost his seat in the national body. The hope then came that he would be appointed Land Office Commissioner of the United States by the newly elected Whig President, Zachary Taylor. They would live in Washington. Lincoln wrote letters, pulled wires, used connections, traveled to Washington, went the limit as an office seeker. It is not known whether he naturally felt he would enjoy the work of running a federal bureau in the national capital, and that it would be an experience worth his while—or whether his wife spurred him on in the only audacious effort he ever put forth for an appointive office. The job was landed by another man. It was not cheerful news at the Lincoln home in Springfield. Lincoln took up mathematics for its mental discipline and sunk himself deep in law study and practice.

Four babies were borne by Mary Todd Lincoln in ten years, all boys, Robert Todd (1843), Edward Baker (1846), William Wallace (1850), Thomas (1853). They made a houseful. Their mother had maids for housework but until the family went to the White House to live, she usually sewed her own dresses, did much of the sewing for the children, and took on herself many of the thousand and one little cares and daily chores that accompany the feeding and clothing of babies, and upbringing of lusty and mischievous boys. She had hours, days, years of washing and nursing these little ones, tending their garments, overseeing their school studies, watching their behavior, instructing them as to the manners of gentlemen, keeping an eye on their health, working and worrying over them when they were sick. Even those who could not see her as pleasant company, even the ones who believed her a vixen and a shrew, gave testimony that she was an exceptional mother, brooding over her offspring with a touch of the tigress.

Her little Eddy died in 1850, not quite four years old; that was a grief. Thomas, nicknamed Tad, had a misshapen palate and lisped; he had brightness, whimsical bold humor; he was a precious burden to his mother and father.

Mrs. Lincoln knew that her husband understood her faults. She believed she knew his failings and instructed him. Across their twenty-two years of married life there were times when she was a help. Often too she knew she presumed on his patience and good nature, knowing that when calm settled down on the household he would regard it as "a little explosion" that had done her good. In the matter of faults she may have heard him tell of meeting a farmer who wanted Lincoln to bring suit against a next-door neighbor. And Lincoln suggested that the farmer should forget it; neighbors are like horses; they all have faults and there is a way of accommodating yourself to the faults you know and expect; trading a horse whose faults you are used to for one who has a new and a different set of faults may be a mistake. Undoubtedly Lincoln had a theory that a turbulent woman and an unruly horse must be met with a patience much the same for either the woman or the horse.

She terrorized housemaids, icemen, storekeepers, delivery boys, with her tongue lashings. He knew these tempers of hers connected directly with the violent headaches of which she complained for many years.

67

He knew they traced back to a deep-seated physical disorder, sudden disturbances that arose and shook her controls till she raved and was as helpless as a child that has spent itself in a tantrum. Sentences of letters she wrote show that she felt guilty and ashamed over her outbreaks of hysteria; she wished they had never happened, felt deeply that she had made a fool of herself. If Lincoln ever suspected that these habitual brainstorms were the result of a cerebral disease eating deeper into the tissues from year to year, it is not revealed in any letter or spoken comment in the known record.

In the courting days and in the earlier years of marriage his nickname for her was "Molly." After the children came he called her "Mother." When complaints were raised against her he tried to smooth out the trouble, telling one man who had been tongue-lashed that he ought to be able to stand for fifteen minutes what he [Lincoln] had stood for fifteen years. Much can be inferred from a letter he wrote to the editor of a new Republican newspaper which Mrs. Lincoln had thrown out of the house in a huff. "When the paper was brought to my house," he explained, "my wife said to me, 'Now are you going to take another worthless little paper?' I said to her *evasively,* 'I have not directed

68

"HOW MUCH, I WISH INSTEAD OF WRITING WE WERE TOGETHER THIS EVENING. I FEEL VERY SAD AWAY FROM YOU"

(In the collection of Oliver R. Barrett)

From an affectionate, domestic letter written by Mrs. Lincoln to her husband when he was a Congressman in 1848.

RARELY DID THE
CAMERA FIND MRS.
LINCOLN WITHOUT
HER FAVORITE
FLOWERS

the paper to be left.' From this, in my absence, she sent the message to the carrier."

Did she on one occasion chase him out of the house with a broomstick? One woman told of it years afterward. It may have been so, though no other witness has come forward to tell about it, and the next-door neighbors, the Gourleys, recalled no affair of the broomstick. "I think the Lincolns agreed moderately well," said James Gourley. "As a rule Mr. Lincoln yielded to his wife—in fact, almost any other man, had he known the woman as I did, would have done the same thing. She was gifted with an unusually high temper and that usually got the better of her. She was very excitable and when wrought up had hallucinations." Once she was afraid of rough characters doing violence to her and the maid. Her wailing brought Gourley over and he spent the night guarding the house. "The whole thing was imaginary," said Gourley. Though others living farther away emphasized her bad peculiarities, Gourley declared, "I never thought Mrs. Lincoln was as bad as some people here in Springfield represented her." When one of her spells of temper came on Lincoln at first seemed to pay no attention. "Frequently he would laugh at her, which is a risky thing to do in the face of an infuriated wife;

but generally, if her impatience continued, he would pick up one of the children and deliberately leave home as if to take a walk. After he had gone, the storm usually subsided, but sometimes it would break out again when he returned."

Did she throw a bucket of water on his head from a second-story window as he stood at the front door asking to be let in? Such a tale has been told and was once published in a foreign language newspaper— printed as fun for the readers who for years laughed at one stage jester asking another, "Who was that lady I seen you with last night?" "That wasn't no lady; that was my wife." There are legends which grow by what they feed on. Possibly once during the eighteen or nineteen years of the married life of the Lincolns in Springfield she threw a bucket of water on him at the front door—possibly once—though Herndon and others never heard of it.

Though the talk and the testimony blame the woman chiefly there seems to have been one time that the man too lost his control. Lincoln was at the office one morning before Herndon arrived. His hat over his eyes he gave a short answer to Herndon's "Good morning," sat slumped till noon, and then made a meal of crackers and cheese. On the day before, on a Sunday morning, Mrs. Lincoln was in a bad mood, one thing led to another and after repeated naggings Lincoln took hold of her and pushed her toward an open door facing Jackson Street, calling in his peculiar high-pitched voice, "You make the house intolerable, damn you, get out of it!" Churchgoers coming up Jackson Street might have seen and heard all. How would they know it was the first and only time in his life he had laid rough hands on his wife and cursed her? Even letting it pass that people had seen and heard what happened how could he blame himself enough for letting himself go in such cheap behavior? So Sunday had been a day of shameful thoughts. The night had brought no sleep. And at daybreak he had come to the law office, without breakfast, without hope.

The marriage contract is complex. "Live and let live," is one of its terms. It travels on a series of readjustments to the changes of life recurring in the party of the first part and the party of the second part. Geared to incessant ecstasy of passion, the arrangement goes smash. Mutual ambitions, a round of simple and necessary duties, occasional or frequent separations as the case may be, relieved by interludes of warm affection—these are the conditions on which many a long-time marriage has been negotiated. The mood and color of this normal married life permeate the letters that passed between Lincoln and his wife when he was in Congress. Their household talk across the twenty-two years must have run along many a day and hour in the mood of these letters; exchanges of news, little anxieties about the children and the home, the journeyings of each reported to the other. When he hurried home from the law office during a thunderstorm, knowing that she was a terror-struck and sick woman during a thunderstorm, it was an act of accommodation by one partner for another. Likewise when a man appeared at the office saying the wife wanted a tree in their home yard cut down, it was accommodation again in his saying, "Then for God's sake let it be cut down!"

All romance is interrupted by the practical. The most passionate of lovers must either go to a hotel or set up housekeeping. And either is a humdrum piece of business in a sheer romance. Many a woman has said, "I love you, but the roast is burning and we must leave our kisses till after dinner." Managing a family and household is the work and care of a husband and wife as distinguished from two lovers. The husband must attend to the "husbandry," the bread-and-butter supply, while his wife loves, cherishes and obeys him; that

72

is the theory; an ancient Saxon verb has it that she "wifes" him. We know from the 1848 letters of Lincoln and his wife that he was husbanding their resources and that she "wifed" him.

We can be sure, too, that for much of the time Lincoln and his wife went about their concerns peacefully and with quiet affection for each other. Domestic flare-ups, nerve-snappings, come to all couples; perhaps to these two they simply came more frequently and more violently. Authentic records—letters written without any thought of future readers—contain many glimpses of placid relations. One can read nothing but calm contentment into Lincoln's sentence about a novel he had received from a friend: "My wife got hold of the volume I took home, read it half through last night, and is greatly interested in it." Only the comradeship that comes to those who understand each other can be inferred from Mrs. Lincoln's comment on a trip east: "When I saw the large steamers at the New York landings I felt in my heart inclined to sigh that poverty was my portion. How I long to go to Europe. I often laugh and tell Mr. Lincoln that I am determined my next husband shall be rich."

Together the two shared in the social life of Springfield, entertained and went to parties. The diary of

Orville H. Browning, who spent weeks every year in the capital, refers often to parties which Mr. and Mrs. Lincoln gave or attended. Mrs. Lincoln's letters show the extent of these diversions. "Within the last three weeks," she wrote in 1857, "there has been a party almost every night and some two or three grand fetes are coming off this week." Most pretentious of these, but typical of many others, was Governor Bissell's reception where "a fine brass and string band discoursed most delicious music, and the dancers kept the cotillions filled until a late hour."

As the years passed and Lincoln's fame grew, there came occasional happy outings, brief escapes for Mrs. Lincoln from the routine of keeping house and managing children. There was a trip, with other lawyers, state officers and their wives, over the lines of the Illinois Central Railroad in the summer of 1859. The Springfield newspapers announced the party's departure and the Chicago papers noted the arrival of the travelers, among them the "Hon. A. Lincoln and family," at the Tremont House. Upon their return to Springfield the men bought a gold-headed cane at Chatterton's jewelry store, had their names inscribed upon it, and presented it to the conductor of the train as a token of appreciation.

74

There was another trip the same year when Lincoln went to Ohio to make Republican speeches, taking Mrs. Lincoln and one of the boys with him. The first audience, at Columbus, was small, but as the trip progressed enthusiasm mounted and ever-larger crowds were present to warm Mrs. Lincoln's pride in her husband's reputation. At Cincinnati marchers with bands met them at the station and escorted them to the Burnet house with cannon booming a salute. They stayed two days, spending several pleasant hours with one of Mrs. Lincoln's cousins.

Lincoln's health, his work, his political aims, are told about in a letter which he wrote to his wife in 1860 on the eastern trip that took him to New York for the Cooper Union speech and nine other speeches. This platform work came hard for him and he made clear to Mrs. Lincoln that he was a troubled man and why. While visiting their son Robert, at Exeter, New Hampshire, he wrote her a letter on March 4, saying, "I have been unable to escape this toil. If I had foreseen it, I think I would not have come east at all. The speech at New York, being within my calculation before I started, went off passably well and gave me no trouble whatever. The difficulty was to make nine others, before audiences who had already seen all my ideas in

75

print." Thus he let her know that if his nine other speeches seemed rather poor there was a reason. Neither he nor she knew at that hour how powerful a factor the Cooper Union address would prove in bringing him the nomination for President a few months later. Nor could they guess that a year from the day he wrote this letter he would be taking oath as President at Washington, and again he would be saying in but slightly different words, "I have been unable to escape this toil."

Communications like this have a color not found in the progress of a man and wife whose days are a succession of uninterrupted quarrels. Nevertheless, we know there were terrible interludes. Under the progression of her malady, the hammering wear and tear of the repeated periods of hysteria and hallucinations, there was a fading of a brightness seen in her younger years. Compliments came less often. She lost her "silver tones." More than twenty years after her query, "Why is it that married folks always become so serious?" she wrote querulously, "The weather is so beautiful, why is it, that we cannot feel well?" The days in which she was neither feeling well nor looking well increased. Her sudden angers interrupting a smoothly moving breakfast, her swift wailings in the dark quiet of night time when fears came to possess her—these brought long thoughts to her husband. Did she become to him a manner of symbol—a miniature of the Sea of Life, smooth and shining with promises and then suddenly treacherous and hateful with devastation? We do not know. It may be so. We cannot be sure in such a realm of the deeper undertows that move people into words and acts.

We do know that from year to year there was a growing control in her husband, a strange and more mystic tinting of his spirit. Under the bonds and leashes that wove and tied his life with that of Mary Todd he saw a self-development that became a mystery to his friends. The outstanding trait of him, according to Herndon, was that he was a "learner," raising the question whether he was indeed such a learner that he could apply to the benefit of his own growth the maxim he quoted to Speed from his father, "If you make a bad bargain, hug it all the tighter."

He was a man in whom the stream of motive ran sluggish. Herndon's theory was that Mary Todd often roused him out of sluggishness, out of vague dreams, into definite actions. When his melancholy weighed down and overslaughed his ambition, Mary Todd with her tongue, arguments, reminders, was a "whiplash."

This, of course, is speculation, an attempt to read secrets in development of human personality. Under the patient exterior of Abraham Lincoln lay a turmoil, a vast criss-cross of volcanic currents of which he himself might have had difficulty to tell had he ever tried to unbosom and make clear the play of motives that operated between him and Mary Todd in their twenty-two years of married life.

Pride ran deep in Mary Todd Lincoln, pride of a depth and consuming intensity that might ally it with the pride which the Puritans named as the first of the seven deadly sins.

When Lincoln was defeated for United States Senator from Illinois in 1855, his wife was in the gallery watching the balloting. Lyman Trumbull, a rival of the same party, won. And though Julia Jayne, the wife of Trumbull, had been a bridesmaid at Mary Todd's wedding, and they had joined in writing poetry and letters to the Sangamo *Journal,* it is said that always after Trumbull's election there was coolness between her and her old-time chum.

Her anxiety matched that of her husband when he ran for the United States Senate against Douglas in 1858. She was not one of those wives who wish their husbands to quit the troublous arena of politics. She had a belief in her own skill at politics and found the rôle of adviser fascinating.

Months of exaltation, of life intensified, followed Lincoln's nomination at Chicago. Mary Lincoln was no longer the wife of a small-town lawyer; like her husband, she was a public character. The transformation thrilled her. The newspaper correspondents who thronged to Springfield gave her space in their dispatches. There was keen delight in reading in the New York *Herald* that she was "especially gracious and entertaining," and able to inject "brilliant flashes of wit and good nature" into a political conversation. There was keen delight, too, in meeting men who sought out her husband at the frame house on the corner of Eighth and Jackson streets—men whose names were household words, Salmon P. Chase, Thurlow Weed, Cameron, Carl Schurz, Horace Greeley.

With the election, life for Mary Lincoln was pitched to an even higher key. "She is in fine spirits!" wrote one of her friends a few days after the result was known.

Still and all, it was not so pleasant for her. Western democracy had its own ways, was not always considerate of feelings. On one of the nights of Republican celebration crowds swarmed through the Lincoln residence. They wanted a look at the President-elect and his lady. Sweat-stained shirts crushed elaborate gowns; muddy boots trampled satin slippers. And more than once Mary Lincoln's cheeks flushed as she found herself the object of a stare and overheard the ill-concealed words: "Is that the old woman?"

With Lincoln's inauguration as President of the United States in 1861 she hugged to her heart the gratification of being the First Lady of the Land. Her fond dream had come true, yet for her it was not merely a signal that she was to wife, comfort, cherish the new President and help him carry the load. She took it she was also an adviser, an ex-officio cabinet officer, an auxiliary First Magistrate. From the first she suggested appointments and was vehement as to who should fill this or that place.

Was there need for her to blaze forth with hot comments on important men whom Lincoln had chosen for heavy work? Why in the presence of visitors refer to William H. Seward, named to be Secretary of State, as a "dirty abolition sneak"?

Henry Villard, correspondent of the New York *Herald,* told of a story he had from a man who went to bring Lincoln to the railroad train which was waiting to carry the President-elect to Washington for inauguration. And the man said Lincoln's wife was lying on the floor of their room in the Chenery House raging and convulsive, her apparel disordered, moaning she would not go to Washington until her husband promised to make a certain federal appointment. It was a story—possibly nothing to it and possibly true. In any case it was told by Villard as probably true. That Villard at this time was writing little character sketches of Lincoln and his wife for the New York *Herald,* entirely favorable, filled with well-measured praise and affection, lends color to the story. That Mrs. Lincoln changed her plans and itinerary, and did not leave Springfield on the same train with her husband, may or may not be a circumstance in the incident. That Lincoln made one of the most poignantly moving and melancholy speeches of his career that morning just before the train carried him away from Springfield forever may also be no circumstance at all.

Was it a woman's jealousy of her husband or a selfish personal pride or both that brought her decree regarding White House promenades? The established custom followed by Presidents and Presidents' wives up till her time was that the President should lead the grand march with another woman on his arm while the next couple would be the President's wife on the arm of another man. Mary Todd Lincoln decreed that she and she only should be the woman on the President's arm when he led the promenade. No other woman but her

INAUGURATION BALL COSTUMES, EVENING OF MARCH 4, 1861

should be in the First Couple. And it was so ordered and maintained from then on.

She is credited with pluck for staying at the White House with her husband and children through the Spring days of 1861 when it seemed as though Washington would be captured, when the Confederates could easily have taken the Capitol and White House. She refused to travel north to Philadelphia and safety.

She had resources of courage; not stamina particularly but a steady audacity.

The Washington tumult wore heavily on her in the Summer of 1861. She went to Long Branch, the ocean resort near New York City. There she conducted herself quietly, trying to rest, keeping away from the social whirl. The New York *Herald,* however, had sent a clever special writer to the scene; he scribbled columns of gush as though the President's wife were an American Queen, maintaining a royal seclusion, wearing a haughty manner. The keen thrusts and malicious manipulations of this writer were reprinted in newspapers fighting the administration. The ridicule went beyond her and struck at her husband in the White House. She learned what curious twists of viewpoint can be put upon a lonely distracted woman seeking a place to look at the wide ocean in peace and meditation; it couldn't be done.

She became a topic. "Mrs. Lincoln held a brilliant levee at the White House on Saturday evening. She was superbly dressed." Thus *Leslie's Weekly* in February of 1863. The same periodical in its number of October 10 that year gave its readers a brief item: "The reports that Mrs. Lincoln was in an interesting condition are untrue."

A bold agitator for abolition and woman's rights, Jane Grey Swisshelm, editor of a paper at St. Cloud, Minnesota, and later a war nurse, gave out words of high admiration and deep affection for Mrs. Lincoln. The words were seized on. *Leslie's Weekly* quoted them: "Her complexion is fair as that of a young girl, her cheeks soft, plump and blooming, and her expression tender and kindly. It was one of those faces I feel like stopping on the street to kiss, because it recalls one that was dearest of all in childhood's days. I think the features are not classical, but I forget them. It was a pleasant face to look on." To this *Leslie's* added: "The Boston *Courier* spitefully reminds its readers that Mrs. Swisshelm is an office-holder. No one can doubt Mrs. Swisshelm's womanly earnestness who remembers the fierce war she waged with Harriet Prewett of the Yazoo *Gazette*, about the weight of their respective babies." Thus she met persiflage, bantering. Or again she was the topic of strict news information as when in July of 1863, journals carried the item: "Mrs. Lincoln nearly met with a fatal accident in consequence of her horses taking fright. She threw herself out of her carriage. Fortunately no bones were broken, and after some restorative she was taken to her residence."

84

I fancy the "Blue room", will look dreary this evening, so if you & the Gov are disengaged, wander up & see us — I want to become accustomed to vast solitude by degrees. The paper is ready for your notice — Bring the Gov — with you —

Truly your friend

Mary Lincoln

"I WANT TO BECOME ACCUSTOMED TO VAST SOLITUDE BY DEGREES," WRITES MRS. LINCOLN EARLY IN 1861

(In the collection of Oliver R. Barrett)

MARY LINCOLN

From a painting by Frank B. Carpenter, White House resident in 1864
and author of "Six Months in the White House." An idealized portrait exe-
cuted some time after the war. (Courtesy of The Milch Galleries, New York)

A steady parade of items about her three "brothers" in the Confederate armies was published in southern and northern newspapers. They were in fact half-brothers, sons of Mary Todd's father by his second wife.

"The Rebel officer who called the roll of our prisoners at Houston is Lieutenant Todd, a brother of the wife of President Lincoln," ran a newspaper line. "He is tall, fat, and savage against the 'Yankees.'" Journals for and against the Lincoln administration reprinted, in December of 1863, information from the Richmond *Enquirer* reading: "Mrs. Todd of Kentucky, the mother of Mrs. Lincoln, arrived in this city on the steamer *Schultz,* Thursday night, having come to City Point on the flag of truce boat. She goes South to visit her daughter, Mrs. Helm, widow of Surgeon-General Helm, who fell at Chickamauga. Mrs. Todd is about to take up her residence South, all her daughters being here, except the wife of Lincoln, and Mrs. Kellogg, who is at present in Paris."

The talk grew and spread that in the White House was a woman traitor and spy, the President's wife, sending information south. On one occasion the sad-faced President appeared of his own volition before a Congressional investigating committee to give them his solemn personal assurance that his wife was loyal to the Union cause.

One by one the Todd brothers in the Confederate army were killed. And little by little the talk died down that their half-sister in the White House was an informer in sympathy with the southern side.

It was war.

"Lizzie, I have just heard that one of my brothers has been killed," said Mrs. Lincoln one day to her negro dressmaker, Elizabeth Keckley. And she went on, "Of course, it is but natural that I should feel for one so nearly related to me, but not to the extent that you suppose. He made his choice long ago. He decided against my husband, and through him against me. He has been fighting against us; and since he chose to be our deadly enemy, I see no special reason why I should bitterly mourn his death."

The tension of being a Kentuckian at war with the South was in her plea, "Why should I sympathize with the rebels? They would hang my husband tomorrow if it was in their power, and perhaps gibbet me with him. How then can I sympathize with a people at war with me and mine?"

Broken aristocrats, southern sympathizers, disgruntled office seekers, gossips shaken with war brainstorms, employed their tongues on the new social leader of the capital, the new First Lady. And she gave them too many chances to strike at her. More than rumor and passing chatter lay back of Charles Francis Adams, Jr.'s recording of a function he attended at Mrs. Eames's: "If the President caught it at dinner, his wife caught it at the reception. All manner of stories about her were flying around; she wanted to do the right thing, but, not knowing how, was too weak and proud to ask; she was going to put the White House on an economic basis, and, to that end, was about to dismiss 'the help,' as she called the servants; some of whom, it was asserted, had already left because 'they must live with gentlefolks'; she had got hold of newspaper reporters and railroad conductors, as the best persons to go to for advice and direction. Numberless stories of this sort were current; and Mrs. Lincoln was in a stew."

In the White House she was sometimes designated as "Mrs. President." She took an interest in the case of a soldier who was sentenced to face a firing squad for going to sleep on picket duty. When Lincoln mentioned the case to General George B. McClellan, commanding, he said "the Lady President" was anxious the boy be pardoned. McClellan in writing to his wife told

.When I was a member of Congress a dozen years ago, I boarded with the lady. who writes the within letter. She is a most worthy, and deserving lady; and if what she desires can be conveniently done, I shall be much obliged I say this sincerely and earnestly —

May 31. 1861

A. Lincoln

Hon Mr Smith:

We boarded some months, with Mrs Sprigg, & found her a most estimable lady & would esteem it a personal favor, if her request, could be granted.

Mrs A. Lincoln

UNUSUAL INSTANCE OF THE HANDWRITINGS OF MR. AND
MRS. LINCOLN ON ONE PAGE

her it had pleased him to grant a request from "the Lady President."

In her own eyes she was more than "the Lady President"; she conceived of her position as carrying with it prerogatives and privileges akin to those of royalty. She was fond of referring to those who frequented the White House as the "Court," and at times she made requests, forced exactions, as one who ruled by monarchic decree and whim rather than as the wife of an elected President. There was the case of Mrs. Taft's bonnet, trivial but characteristic. After one of the Marine Band concerts Julia Taft and her mother went to the portico of the White House to pay their respects to Mrs. Lincoln. "I noticed Mrs. Lincoln looking intently at my mother's bonnet," the daughter recorded. "After a few words of greeting, she took my mother aside and talked with her for a moment. While I could not hear their conversation, I knew someway that they were talking about my mother's bonnet and I was a bit puzzled at the look of amazement on my mother's face. I did not see why my mother should look so surprised at a passing compliment from Mrs. Lincoln." That evening she overheard scraps of a guarded conversation between her mother and father: learned that the milliner who had made Mrs. Taft's bonnet had also made one for Mrs. Lincoln but had not had enough ribbon for the strings, and that Mrs. Lincoln had asked her mother for those from her own bonnet. The daughter concluded: "It was an outstanding characteristic of Mary Todd Lincoln that she wanted what she wanted when she wanted it and no substitute!"

Seward, whom Mrs. Lincoln disliked and sought to replace with Sumner, recognized the trait and bowed to it. When Mrs. Lincoln asked Attorney General Speed to go to City Point with her early in April, 1865, Speed, behind in his work, demurred and consulted Seward. Whereupon, in Speed's words, his colleague "arose and walked the floor, and said with great emphasis, the request of the President's wife was equivalent to a command, and you must obey." And Speed went.

She intervened constantly in the matter of offices—for postmasterships, West Point cadetships—even the reorganization of the Cabinet. She wrote from the Soldiers' Home, Washington, D. C., to James Gordon Bennett, publisher and editor of the New York *Herald* in the fall of 1862, telling him she favored cabinet changes and would do what she could to bring them about:

"From all parties the cry for a 'change of cabinet' comes. I hold a letter, just received from Governor Sprague, in my hand, who is quite as earnest as you have been on the subject. Doubtless if my good patient husband were here instead of being with the Army of the Potomac, both of these missives would be placed before him, accompanied by my womanly suggestions, proceeding from a heart so deeply interested for our distracted country. I have a great terror of strong-minded ladies, yet if a word fitly spoken and in due season can be urged in a time like this, we should not withhold it."

Her jealousies of other women who seemed in the slightest to be in favor with the President were noticeable. Mrs. Keckley recorded the conversation of one evening as Lincoln was pulling on his gloves in Mrs. Lincoln's room just before escorting her to a reception downstairs in the White House. With a twinkle in his eyes he remarked, "Well, mother, who must I talk with tonight—shall it be Mrs. D.?"

"That deceitful woman! No, you shall not listen to her flattery."

"Well, then, what do you say to Miss C.? She is too young and handsome to practice deceit."

"Young and handsome, you call her! You shall not

judge beauty for me. No, she is in league with Mrs.
D., and you shall not talk with her."

"Well, mother, I must talk with some one. Is there
any one that you do not object to?" And he fussed at
buttoning a glove, a mock gravity on his face.

"I don't know as it is necessary you should talk to
anybody in particular. You know well enough, Mr.
Lincoln, that I do not approve of your flirtations with
silly women, just as if you were a beardless boy, fresh
from school."

"But, mother, I insist that I must talk with some-
body. I can't stand around like a simpleton, and say
nothing. If you will not tell me who I may talk with,
please tell me who I may *not* talk with."

"There is Mrs. D. and Miss C. in particular, I detest
them both. Mrs. B. also will come around you, but you
need not listen to her flattery. These are the ones in
particular."

"Very well, mother; now that we have settled the
question to your satisfaction, we will go downstairs."
And he gave her his arm.

One evening Mrs. Keckley had arranged Mrs. Lincoln's hair and helped her into a dress of white satin
trimmed in black lace, with a surprise of a long trail
in the height of daring fashion. She entered the Guest's

Room where Willie Lincoln lay abed with a cold and fever. And as Elizabeth Keckley wrote of it, "As she swept through the room, Mr. Lincoln was standing with his back to the fire, his hands behind him, and his eyes on the carpet. His face wore a thoughtful, solemn look. The rustling of the satin dress attracted his attention. He looked at it a few moments; then, in his quaint, quiet way remarked—

" 'Whew! Our cat has a long tail tonight!'

"Mrs. Lincoln did not reply. The President added:

" 'Mother, it is my opinion, if some of that tail was nearer the head, it would be in better style'; and he glanced at her bare arms and neck. She had a beautiful neck and arm and low dresses were becoming to her. She turned away with a look of offended dignity, and presently took the President's arm, and both went downstairs to their guests, leaving me alone with the sick boy."

The cup of happiness ran over for Mary Todd Lincoln at times when she realized to the full her ambition to be a Great Lady and publicly approved as such. Praise was showered on her and lavish compliments bestrewn over her after the White House party which she gave on February 5, 1862. *Leslie's Weekly* made this social function the topic of a leading article, elab-

orately illustrated. "There has been a social innovation
at the White House," the article began, "and the experi-
ment has been a brilliant success." Until this event came
off there had been "a false deference to the false no-
tion of democratic equality." Except for State dinners
to foreign ministers and cabinet members the parties
previously had consisted of public receptions where the
Executive Mansion was thrown open, as *Leslie's
Weekly* noted, "to every one, high or low, gentle or
ungentle, washed or unwashed," resulting in a "horrible jam" endurable only "by people of sharp elbows,
and destitute of corns, who don't object to a faint odor
of whiskey." Now, however, Mrs. Lincoln had inaugu-
rated the practice of "respectable people in private life"
by inviting five hundred of the "distinguished, beautiful, brilliant" people representing "intellect, attainment,
position, elegance." Whether the writer in *Leslie's* was
lit up with genuine enthusiasm or was just a plain
snob, he or she wrote as though conveying glad tidings.
"Indeed, no European Court or capital can compare
with the Presidential circle and the society at Washington this winter, in the freshness and beauty of its
women. The North, while it has confessedly been possessed of even more than its numerical proportion of
beautiful and accomplished women, has never before

been in a social supremacy. The power which controlled the Government has been altogether Southern, and society has always taken the same hue. But all that is changed now, and the dingy, sprawling city on the Potomac is bright with the blue of Northern eyes, and the fresh, rosy glow of Northern complexions." Early in the evening the windows of the White House were lighted for gayety, and by half-past nine the entrances were crowded with guests and carriages lined the White House yard to the avenue. Invitation cards were presented at the door. The ladies in swishing, crinkling crinoline and their escorts in silk top hats and cutaway coats passed to the second-story dressing rooms. They returned to the grand entrance, were shown into the Blue Room, then conducted to the grand saloon or East Room where the President and his wife greeted them while the Marine Band played soft music from a side-room. At half-past eleven doors were thrown open to an apartment where sandwiches were served with drinks from a huge Japanese punchbowl. The regular supper came afterwards, served by Maillard of New York in the Dining Room. The reporter noted that Mrs. John J. Crittenden's jewels were diamonds, her gown of black velvet, richly trimmed with lace, while her head-dress was composed of crimson flowers. Also the wife of Gen. George B. McClellan, "the observed of all observers, leaning on the arm of her distinguished husband, looked most regal in her dress of white, with bands of cherry velvet, a tunic of white looped with crimson, and a head-dress of white illusion, *a la vierge.*" Mrs. Commodore Levy was there, "most bewitchingly *piquante* in a dress of white illusion and gold, with six small flounces over a slip of white glace silk, a wreath of white flowers mingled with golden ears of wheat, and a necklace and earrings of Oriental pearls." It was noted too: "The Hon. Mrs. Squier looked most charming in a pink silk, exquisitely trimmed with swansdown, which well accorded with her soft and *spirituelle* beauty. A wreath of ivy with its long and graceful tendrils, mingled most bewitchingly with her blonde and waving hair. Her ornaments were opals and diamonds." Also the reporter for *Leslie's Weekly* recorded: "Mrs. Griffin was simply but tastefully attired in a corn-colored silk; head-dress of bright crimson flowers. She was the observed of all, as she leaned on the arm of the President."

Many were named as present and set off with distinction. But the lavish comment was reserved for Mrs. Lincoln. "Primarily, we must remark the exquisite taste with which the White House has been refitted under Mrs. Lincoln's directions is in no respect more remarkable than in the character of the hangings of the various rooms, which relieve and set off the figures and dresses of lady guests to the greatest advantage. First, as hostess, and second in no respect, Mrs. Lincoln. She was attired in a lustrous white satin robe, with a train of a yard in length, trimmed with one deep flounce of the richest black chantilly lace, put on in festoons and surmounted by a quilling of white satin ribbon, edged with narrow black lace. The dress was, of course, décolleté and with short sleeves, displaying the exquisitely moulded shoulders and arms of our fair 'Republican Queen,' the whiteness of which were absolutely dazzling. Her head-dress was a coronet wreath of black and white crêpe myrtle, which was in perfect keeping with her regal style of beauty. Let us here add *en passant,* that Mrs. Lincoln possesses that rare beauty which has rendered the Empress of the French so celebrated as a handsome woman, and which our Trans-atlantic cousins call *la tête bien planté.* Her ornaments were pearls."

Such was the presentation of Mrs. Lincoln to the wide national audience of a popular illustrated weekly newspaper. She had wanted this recognition. It slaked a thirst she had. Later that same year, in November,

New York newspapers gave many paragraphs to her visit there. But it was not so pleasant a visit. For the Lincoln administration at Washington had been losing ground and the end of the war seemed far off. *Harper's Weekly* published a large engraving from a photograph portrait of Mrs. Lincoln, with the news: "Mrs. Lincoln has lately been spending some time in this city, and has been serenaded and visited by many of our leading citizens." Along with this was the information that one of her brothers, killed in battle, had been the jailer of Union prisoners at Richmond. "His brutality and cruelty were such, however, that Jefferson Davis finally removed him from the post, and sent him to join his regiment. Mrs. Lincoln's sisters are understood to sympathize rather with the rebels than with the Government. It is probably this division of sentiment which has given rise to the gossip and scandal respecting the views of the lady who presides over the White House."

At one time newspapers and common talk were filled with accusations and suspicions that she was getting military secrets from her husband and White House callers, and sending the information to Southern commanders. She told the White House clerk who handled mail, William O. Stoddard, that she would prefer he opened all her mail as it came. "Don't let a thing come to me that you've not read first yourself, and that you are not sure I would wish to see. I do not wish to open a letter, nor even a parcel of any kind,

To
Taddie Lincoln
from his loving
Mother
Dec 4ᵗʰ 63

MRS. LINCOLN INSCRIBES A GIFT TO HER SON
In the collection of Oliver R. Barrett

until after you have examined it. Never!" Stoddard took it on himself to throw into the waste basket and the fireplace many accusing and threatening letters addressed to her, written by persons Stoddard considered "insane and depraved."

In all the representations of the gossips, however, there was never an intimation during war time that she

99

mistreated her children. A story that she had whipped Tad came later—and was on the face of it a malicious fabrication. She was fond of her young ones, and if anything, overindulged them. And something of this mother heart was stirred into action as the train-loads of broken and battered soldiers were unloaded at Washington fresh from the battlefields. Much that she did was worthy of her place and her own best impulses. Day after day she visited the wounded in the Washington hospitals, talked with them, took them fruit and delicacies, wine and liquors that admirers had sent for the use of the White House table. In her own way she tried to lighten the burden her husband was carrying. She invited old Illinois friends to breakfast at the White House so that he might forget himself for a few moments in talk of old times. She made him ride with her on bright afternoons in the hope that an hour or two of fresh air would blot some of the fatigue from his face.

A different reputation might have been built up for her, W. O. Stoddard, the mail clerk, believed, if she had taken pains now and then to have the newspaper correspondents know of her hospital visits, her donations of supplies, and other good works. Yet even to Stoddard, who wanted to overlook her faults, she was

MRS. LINCOLN
READY FOR THE
INAUGURAL BALL

THE LADY OF THE
WHITE HOUSE, SOME-
TIMES ALLUDED TO AS
"MRS. PRESIDENT"

War time card portraits of Mrs. Lincoln widely published in periodicals
and treasured in family albums throughout the north.
(Originals in Illinois State Historical Library)

FOUR PICTURES OF MRS. LINCOLN WIDELY CIRCULATED DURING
WAR TIME

difficult. "It was not easy, at first," he wrote, "to understand why a lady who could be one day so kindly, so considerate, so generous, so thoughtful and so hopeful, could, upon another day, appear so unreasonable, so irritable, so despondent, so even niggardly, and so prone to see the dark, the wrong side of men and women and events."

On a chilly day in February, 1862, Willie Lincoln had gone riding on his pony and taken a cold that passed into fever. He was twelve years old, a blue-eyed boy, not strong, liked his books, sometimes curled up in a chair with pencil and paper and tried his hand at writing poems. One verse of his piece titled "Lines on the Death of Colonel Edward Baker" read:

"There was no patriot like Baker,
    So noble and so true;
He fell as a soldier on the field,
    His face to the sky of blue."

As he lay that night breathing rather hard there drifted up to the room the fragments of music from the Marine Band playing in the Ball Room below. Though the doctor had said there was no reason for alarm about the patient the President had ordered no dancing for that evening. Several times Mrs. Lincoln left the party below and came upstairs to stand over Willie's bed and see how he was.

A few days later the mystic and inevitable messenger came for the boy. Elizabeth Keckley wrote: "The light faded from his eyes, and the death-dew gathered on his brow." She had been on watch but did not see the end, telling of it, "I was worn out with watching, and was not in the room when Willie died, but was immediately sent for. I assisted in washing him and dressing him, and then laid him on the bed, when Mr. Lincoln came in." He lifted the cover from the face of his child, gazed at it long, and murmured, "It is hard, hard to have him die."

The mother wept for hours, and at moments moaned in convulsions of grief.

They closed down the lids over the blue eyes of the boy, parted his brown hair, put flowers from his mother in his pale, crossed hands, and soldiers, senators, the cabinet officers, ambassadors, came to the funeral. The mother couldn't come. She was too far spent.

The body was sent west to Illinois for burial. And the mother clutched at his memory and if his name was mentioned her voice shook and the tears came. "She could not bear to look upon his picture," said Mrs. Keckley. "And after his death she never crossed the threshold of the Guest's Room in which he died, or the Green Room in which he was embalmed."

The death of Willie gave impetus to the malady gnawing at her brain. Noah Brooks told how a charlatan named Colchester posed as a spiritualistic medium, induced her to receive him at the Soldiers' Home and in a darkened room pretended to receive messages from the dead boy. Brooks revealed the fraud. She turned to others for revelations. In amazement Orville H. Browning recorded in his diary: "Mrs. Lincoln told me she had been, the night before, with old Isaac Newton, out to Georgetown, to see a Mrs. Laury, a spiritualist and she had made wonderful revelations to her about her little son Willie who died last winter, and also about things on the earth. Among other things she revealed that the cabinet were all enemies of the President, working for themselves, and that they would have to be dismissed, and others called to his aid before he had success."

Mary Lincoln was a woman who had never restrained her emotions, had all her life given way to gusts of anger and temper. When grief came, it shook her with irresistible force. Mrs. Keckley told of a scene. "In one of her paroxysms of grief the President bent kindly over his wife, took her by the arm, and gently

TEXT OF TELEGRAM OF MRS. LINCOLN, AN INSTANCE OF HER HURRIED LARGE-LETTERED SCRIPT IN MARKED CONTRAST WITH HER CUSTOMARY PRECISE HANDWRITING   *Collection of Oliver R. Barrett* led her to the window. With a stately, solemn gesture, he pointed to the lunatic asylum. 'Mother, do you see that large white building on the hill yonder? Try and control your grief, or it will drive you mad, and we may have to send you there.' "

She was one of those who in their misery cannot realize that sympathy is a short-lived plant, that with the world at large pity shades quickly into resentment at sustained sorrow. In the summer of 1863 Gideon Welles found it necessary to speak to Lincoln about the weekly concerts of the Marine Band, which had been discontinued the previous summer after Mrs. Lincoln had protested. Lincoln said that his wife would not consent to a resumption of the concerts, certainly not until after the Fourth of July. Welles pressed the point: the people had grumbled last year, and would grumble more if the concerts were not resumed. He wrote in his diary: "The public will not sympathize in sorrows which are obtrusive and assigned as a reason for depriving them of enjoyments to which they have been accustomed, and it is a mistake to persist in it."

The war years pounded on. McClellan, whom Mrs. Lincoln epitomized as a "humbug," was eventually replaced by Ulysses S. Grant. "He is a butcher," she told her husband as Grant was moving slowly and at terrible cost toward Richmond. "But he has been very successful in the field," argued the President, as Mrs. Keckley heard it. Mrs. Lincoln responded, "Yes, he generally manages to claim a victory, but such a victory! He loses two men to the enemy's one. He has no management, no regard for life. If the war should continue four years longer, and he should remain in power, he would depopulate the North. I could fight an army as well myself. According to his tactics, there is nothing under the heavens to do but to march a new line of men up in front of the rebel breastworks to be shot down as fast as they take their position, and keep marching until the enemy grows tired of the slaughter. Grant, I repeat, is an obstinate fool and a butcher."

"Well, mother," came the President's slow and ironical voice, "supposing that we give you command of the army. No doubt you would do much better than any general that has been tried."

In the spring of 1864 the President and Mrs. Lincoln went to City Point for a visit with Grant's army. Adam Badeau of Grant's staff was riding in an ambulance with Mrs. Lincoln and Mrs. Grant and happened in the course of talk to say that the wives of army officers at the front had been ordered to the rear. This indicated that lively fighting was soon to begin, a sure sign,

Badeau remarked, for not a lady had been allowed to stay at the front except Mrs. Griffin, the wife of General Charles Griffin, who had a special permit from the President.

"What do you mean by that, sir?" came the cry from Mrs. Lincoln. "Do you mean to say that she saw the President alone? Do you know that I never allow the President to see any woman alone?"

Badeau tried to tone down what he had said. "I tried to palliate my remark," he noted later. And in doing so he smiled some sort of a smile which brought from the raging woman the reply, "That's a very equivocal smile, sir. Let me out of this carriage at once. I will ask the President if he saw that woman alone." She told Badeau in the front seat, to have the driver of the ambulance stop. He hesitated. She thrust her arms past Badeau and took hold of the driver. Mrs. Grant at that point managed to quiet Mrs. Lincoln enough to have the whole party set out on the ground. General George G. Meade now came up and paid his respects to the President's wife. She went off on the arm of the Gettysburg commander before Badeau could give Meade the word that he mustn't mention Mrs. Griffin getting a special permit from the President to stay at the front. Later, however, Badeau saluted Meade as a diplomat, for when Meade and Mrs. Lincoln returned she said to Badeau, "General Meade is a gentleman, sir. He says it was not the President who gave Mrs. Griffin the permit, but the Secretary of War." And when Badeau and Mrs. Grant talked over the day's events they agreed it was all so mixed-up and disgraceful they would neither of them ever mention to anybody what had happened, except that she would tell her husband.

The next day was worse. For it happened that the wife of General Ord, commander of the Army of the James, was not subject to the order retiring wives to the rear, and mounted on a horse suddenly found herself riding alongside President Lincoln, with Mrs. Lincoln and Mrs. Grant in an ambulance just behind them. Mrs. Lincoln caught sight of them and raged. "What does this woman mean by riding by the side of the President? and ahead of me? Does she suppose that *he* wants *her* by the side of him?"

Mrs. Grant did her best to quiet the frenzied woman. Then she came in for a tongue-lashing, in the midst of which Mrs. Lincoln flashed out, "I suppose you think you'll get to the White House yourself, don't you?" Mrs. Grant replied she was satisfied where she was; she had greater honor than she had ever expected to reach.

"Oh!" was the reply. "You had better take it if you can get it. 'Tis very nice."

Major Seward, a nephew of the Secretary of State, now came riding alongside the ambulance and tried for a joke. He didn't know what was going on. It seemed all in the day's gayety for him to call out: "The President's horse is very gallant, Mrs. Lincoln. He insists on riding by the side of Mrs. Ord." The wild cry came, "What do you mean by that, sir?" And the young major's horse began acting fractious and he dropped to the rear.

The trip ended. Mrs. Ord came to the ambulance and suddenly found herself facing a storm of insults, epithets and dirty names, before a crowd of army officers. What did she mean by following the President? And Badeau wrote, "The poor woman burst into tears and inquired what she had done, but Mrs. Lincoln refused to be appeased, and stormed till she was tired. Mrs. Grant still tried to stand by her friend, and everybody was shocked and horrified."

And the evening of that day was worse yet. On a steamer in the James River at a dinner given by President and Mrs. Lincoln to General and Mrs. Grant and the General's staff, Mrs. Lincoln openly and baldly before all suggested that General Ord should be removed from command. He was unfit for his place, to say nothing of his wife. General Grant, of course, had to reply that so far as he could see General Ord was a good commander.

During this City Point visit these outbreaks of Mary Todd Lincoln kept on. And according to Badeau, "Mrs. Lincoln repeatedly attacked her husband in the presence of officers because of Mrs. Griffin and Mrs. Ord . . . He bore it as Christ might have done; with an expression of pain and sadness that cut one to the heart, but with supreme calmness and dignity. He called her 'mother,' with his old-time plainness; he pleaded with eyes and tones, and endeavored to explain or palliate the offenses of others, till she turned on him like a tigress; and then he walked away, hiding that noble, ugly face that we might not catch the full expression of its misery."

One night toward the end of the war Richard J. Oglesby rode in a carriage with President and Mrs. Lincoln. As a brigadier at Corinth Oglesby received wounds it took him a year to recover from, and Lincoln had wired Grant saying Oglesby was an "intimate friend" and he wished news of his wounded associate in Illinois law and politics. And after the carriage ride that night in Washington, Oglesby told an Illinois crony, a responsible friend with whom he sometimes talked and drank all night, just what had happened. This friend gave Oglesby's version of what happened in these words:

"Oglesby went with a committee to get Lincoln to speak at a mass meeting in the interests of the sanitary fair commission. Lincoln said he was all tired out; he ought not to go; he needed rest. But they kept pressing him about how important it was till at last he said he would go if they would pledge him he wouldn't have to speak. They said the main point was that he should be present personally and he wouldn't be required to speak. So, that night Oglesby and the President and Mrs. Lincoln got into a carriage and rode to the meeting. A large crowd was on hand. The chairman introduced the main speaker, whose speech was well received though it was a prepared address. Then there were calls for Lincoln. The chairman told the crowd Lincoln had come with no expectation of delivering an address and they would have to excuse him. But the crowd wouldn't have it that way. They persisted. And at last Lincoln stood up and started to speak. Now Lincoln never was much on short speeches; he generally had some proposition to discuss up and down. And he delivered some remarks, the best he could; it wasn't much of a speech. But the crowd gave him a generous round of applause and were enthusiastic. Then a little later Lincoln and Mrs. Lincoln and Oglesby walked out to the front of the building to meet the carriage. It was a cold evening and the driver had taken the horses around the block to keep them warm. And as the carriage was about to arrive, Mrs. Lincoln broke out in a humiliated and exasperated way, in words like, 'That was the worst speech I ever listened to in my life. How any man could get up and deliver such remarks to an audience is more than I can understand. I wanted the earth to sink and let me go through.' And that was all that was said. The carriage came. The three of them, Lincoln, Mrs. Lincoln, and Oglesby got in and rode to the White House without a word spoken. There Lincoln and Mrs. Lincoln got out without a word, and the carriage drove off to take Oglesby to his quarters. It was a strange incident."

Her speech included frequent use of the word "Sir." Men recalled her overuse of "Sir." Mrs. Keckley several times noted the expression, "God, no!" when Mrs. Lincoln wished to be emphatic in denial.

She spoke to Mrs. Keckley of an "unprincipled set" of politicians with whom she was having dealings in 1864 toward the reëlection of the President in the coming campaign. "Does Mr. Lincoln know what your purpose is?" asked Mrs. Keckley.

"God, no! he would never sanction such proceedings, so I keep him in the dark, and will tell him of it when it is all over. He is too honest to take the proper care of his own interests, so I feel it my duty to electioneer for him."

Henry Villard made note of the "common set of men and women" in whose company she was too often seen. Out of them he singled, for an example of both type and method, the so-called "Chevalier" Wikoff, a handsome, well-mannered, well-educated pretender who was in reality merely a salaried social spy of the New York *Herald*. "Wikoff showed the utmost assurance in his appeals to the vanity of the mistress of the White House," Villard wrote. "I myself heard him compliment her upon her looks and dress in so fulsome a way that she ought to have blushed and banished the impertinent fellow from her presence. She accepted Wikoff as a majordomo in general and in special, as a guide in matters of social etiquette, domestic arrangements, and personal requirements, including her toilette, and as always welcome company for visitors in her salon and on her drives."

Mrs. Keckley told of her impression of the White

113

House couple. "I believe that he loved the mother of his children very tenderly. He asked nothing but affection from her, but did not always receive it. When in one of her wayward, impulsive moods, she was apt to do and say things that wounded him deeply. If he had not loved her, she would have been powerless to cloud his thoughtful face. She often wounded him in unguarded moments, but calm reflection never failed to bring regret." Thus ran the observation of this remarkable mulatto woman who as friend and helper of Mary Todd Lincoln was more notable than any other who tried to smooth her pathway.

One day in 1864 she told Mrs. Keckley that the reelection of Mr. Lincoln was important to her. "Somehow I have learned to fear that he will be defeated. If he should be defeated, I do not know what would become of us all. To me, to him, there is more at stake in this election than he dreams of."

"What can you mean, Mrs. Lincoln?"

"Simply this. I have contracted large debts, of which he knows nothing, and which he will be unable to pay if he is defeated."

"What are your debts, Mrs. Lincoln?"

"They consist chiefly of store bills. I owe altogether about twenty-seven thousand dollars, the principal por-

tion at Stewart's in New York. You understand, Liza-
beth, that Mr. Lincoln has but little idea of the expenses
of a woman's wardrobe. He glances at my rich dresses,
and is happy in the belief that the few hundred dollars I obtain from him supply all my wants. I must
dress in costly materials. The people scrutinize every
article that I wear with critical curiosity. The very fact
of having grown up in the West subjects me to more
searching observation. To keep up appearances I must
have money—more than Mr. Lincoln can spare for me.
I had, and still have, no alternative but to run in debt."

"And Mr. Lincoln does not even suspect how much
you owe?"

"God, no! and I would not have him suspect. The
knowledge would drive him mad. He does not know
a thing about my debt, and I value his happiness, not
to speak of my own, too much to allow him to know
anything. This is what troubles me so much. If he is re-
elected, I can keep him in ignorance of my affairs; but
if he is defeated, then the bills will be sent in, and he
will know all." And having told this, "something like
a hysterical sob escaped her."

Meantime, outside the White House and over the
country the discussion, the talk, the gossip, of four
years about the First Lady of the Land, had gathered

headway. Her reputation had become the sinister crea-
tion of thousands of personal impressions spoken by
people who had seen her or talked with her; of thousands of newspaper items about her coming and going
to Long Branch, Saratoga Springs, Boston, New York,
for rest, for parties and receptions, for shopping; of
hundreds of items about gifts presented to her, her
house, her boys; of hundreds of items of public prints
and private gossip about her gowns and coiffures, her
jewels and adornments; of private information held by
scores of persons in high office who knew of her capri-
ces, tempers, jealousies. The journalist, biographer and
novelist, Mary Clemmer Ames, set forth a viewpoint
common to a large and possibly overwhelming major-
ity of the men and women of the country who held
any definite viewpoint at all. "Wives, mothers and
daughters, in ten thousand homes, were looking into
the faces of husbands, sons and fathers, with trembling
and with tears, and yet with sacrificial patriotism. They
knew, they felt the best-beloved were to be slain on the
country's battlefields. It was the hour for self-forgetting.
Personal vanity and elation, excusable in a more peace-
ful time, seemed unpardonable in this. Yet, in review-
ing the character of Presidents' wives, we shall see that
there was never one who entered the White House with

A PHOTOGRAPH OF
LINCOLN IN 1865,
PROBABLY BY BRADY

*(From the collection of
Frederick H. Meserve)*

"SHE WON'T THINK
ANYTHING ABOUT IT,"
WERE LINCOLN'S
LAST WORDS

CHAIR IN WHICH THE
PRESIDENT SAT WHEN
SHOT BY ASSASSIN

*(From the
Illinois State Historical Library)*

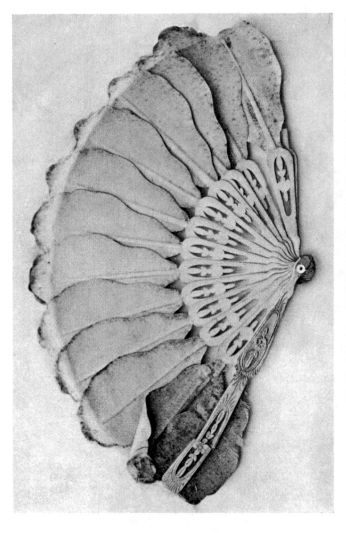

FAN CARRIED BY MRS. LINCOLN ON THE NIGHT OF THE ASSASSINATION—BLOOD-STAINED AND SPOTTED

(In the collection of Oliver R. Barrett)

such a feeling of self-satisfaction, which amounted to personal exultation, as did Mary Lincoln. To her it was the fulfillment of a life-long ambition, and she made her journey to Washington a triumphal passage."

Mary Clemmer Ames wrote what was partly overstatement, partly and in degree a harsh judgment, yet she also reported what was in the heart of numbers of women. "In the distant farm house women waited, breathless, the latest story of battle. In the crowded cities they gathered by thousands, crying, only, 'Let me work for my brother; he dies for me!' With the record of the march and the fight, and of the unseemly defeat, the newspapers teemed with gossip concerning the lady in the White House. While her sister-women scraped lint, sewed bandages, and put on nurses' caps, and gave their all to country and to death, the wife of the President spent her time in rolling to and fro between Washington and New York, intent on extravagant purchases for herself and the White House. Mrs. Lincoln seemed to have nothing to do but to 'shop,' and the reports of her lavish bargains, in the newspapers, were vulgar and sensational in the extreme. The wives and daughters of other Presidents had managed to dress as elegant women, without the process of so doing becoming prominent or public. But not a new dress or jewel was bought by Mrs. Lincoln that did not find its way into the newspapers."

In the White House Mrs. Ames saw "a lonely man, sorrowful at heart, weighed down by mighty burdens"; toiling and suffering alone. Washington had become one vast hospital. "The reluctant river laid at the feet of the city its priceless freight of lacerated men. The wharves were lined with the dying and the dead. One ceaseless procession of ambulances moved to and fro . . . Our streets resounded with the shrieks of the sufferers. Churches, halls and houses were turned into hospitals . . . Through it all Mrs. Lincoln 'shopped.' . . . The nation seemed goaded at last to exasperation. Letters of rebuke, of expostulation, of anathema even, addressed to her, personally, came in to her from every direction. Not a day that did not bring her many such communications, denouncing her mode of life . . . To no other American woman had ever come an equal chance to set a lofty example of self-abnegation to her countrywomen. But just as if there were no national peril, no monstrous national debt, no rivers of blood flowing, she seemed chiefly intent upon pleasure, personal flattery and adulation; upon extravagant dress and ceaseless self-gratification."

The politicians with whom Mrs. Lincoln held interviews and had dealings regarding appointments and nominations, also her extreme household economy, were discussed by thousands in somewhat the words of Mary Clemmer Ames. "Vain, seeking admiration, the men who fed her weakness for their own political ends were sure of her favor. Thus, while daily disgracing the State by her own example, she still sought to meddle in its affairs. Woe to Mr. Lincoln if he did not appoint her favorites. Prodigal in personal expenditures, she brought shame upon the President's House by petty economies, which had never disgraced it before. Had the milk of its dairy been sent to the hospitals, she would have received golden praise. But the whole city felt scandalized to have it haggled over and peddled from the back door of the White House. State dinners could have been dispensed with, without a word of blame, had their cost been consecrated to the soldiers' service; but when it was made apparent that they were omitted from personal penuriousness and a desire to devote their cost to personal gratification, the public censure knew no bounds."

Mary Clemmer Ames reports what happened as a result of the letters that poured in on the Lady President. "From the moment Mrs. Lincoln began to receive recriminating letters, she considered herself an injured individual, the honored object of envy, jealousy and spite, and a martyr to her high position. No doubt some of them were unjust, and many more unkind; but it never dawned upon her consciousness that any part of the provocation was on her side, and after a few tastes of their bitter draughts she ceased to open them."

There came the reëlection of the President in the fall of 1864. There came the night of April 14, 1865, when she was alongside her husband in a box at Ford's Theatre. She sat close to him, leaned on him, as she afterward told it to her friend, Dr. Anson G. Henry. And she was a little afraid her behavior might be embarrassing to the daughter of Senator Harris of Rhode Island sitting near by. She said to the President, "What will Miss Harris think of my hanging on to you so?" "She won't think anything about it." And those were his last words. There came the assassin's bullet. And soon Abraham Lincoln lay on a bed in the back room of the Peterson house across from Ford's Theatre, breathing hard all night long and trying to struggle back to consciousness. His wife sat in the front room weeping, "uttering heartbroken exclamations all night long," leaving the house with the moan, "O my God, and I have given my husband to die!" There came to her such dumb despair as made all pain in her life

FORD'S THEATRE

TENTH STREET, ABOVE E.

SEASON II.... WEEK XXXI.....NIGHT 191
WHOLE NUMBER OF NIGHTS, 496.

JOHN T. FORD................................PROPRIETOR AND MANAGER
(Also of Holliday's St. Theatre, Baltimore, and Academy of Music, Phila
Stage Manager ....J. B. WRIGHT
Treasurer ....H. CLAY FORD

Friday Evening, April 14th, 1865.

THIS EVENING

The Performance will be honored by the presence of

PRESIDENT LINCOLN

BENEFIT

—AND—

LAST NIGHT

OF MISS

LAURA KEENE

THE DISTINGUISHED MANAGERESS AUTHORESS, and ACTRESS

Supported by

MR. JOHN DYOTT

AND

MR. HARRY HAWK

TOM TAYLOR'S CELEBRATED ECCENTRIC COMEDY

As originally produced in America by Miss Keene, and performed by her upwards of

ONE THOUSAND NIGHTS,

ENTITLED

OUR AMERICAN

COUSIN

FLORENCE TRENCHARD......MISS LAURA KEENE
(Her Original Character)

Abel Murcott, Clerk to Attorney	John Dyott
Asa Trenchard	Harry Hawk
Sir Edward Trenchard	T. C. GOURLAY
Lord Dundreary	E. A. EMERSON
Mr. Coyle, Attorney	J. MATTHEWS
Lieutenant Vernon, R. N.	W. J. FERGUSON
Captain De Boots	C. BYRNES
Binney	G. G. SPEAR
Buddicomb, a Valet	H. EVANS
John Whicker, a Gardner	J. L. DeBONAY
Rasper, a Groom	
Bailiff	G. A. PARKHURST and L. JOHNSON
Mary Trenchard	Miss J. GOURLAY
Mrs Mountchessington	Mrs. H. MUZZY
Augusta	Miss M. TRUEMAN
Georgiana	Miss M. HART
Sharpe	Mrs. J. H. EVANS
Skillet	Miss H. GOURLAY

SATURDAY EVENING, APRIL 15.

BENEFIT OF MISS JENNIE GOURLAY

When will be presented BOURCICAULT'S Great Sensational Drama,

THE OCTOROON.

Easter Monday, April 17. Engagement of the YOUNG AMERICAN TRAGEDIAN,

EDWIN ADAMS

FOR TWELVE NIGHTS ONLY.

THE PRICES OF ADMISSION

Orchestra	$1.00
Dress Circle and Parquette	75
Family Circle	25
Private Boxes	$6 and $10

J. R. FORD, Business Manager.

PLAY BILL FOR
FORD'S THEATRE,
NIGHT OF
APRIL 14, 1865

till then seem easy in comparison. The bitterness of the hour was that so few friends could come to speak a word or touch her hand or sit in quiet with her and give her comfort by silent presence. The nearest to a

Green Room.

Admit the Bearer to the
EXECUTIVE MANSION,
On **WEDNESDAY,** *the*
19th of April, 1865.

ADMISSION CARD TO THE FUNERAL SERVICES
AT THE WHITE HOUSE

great friend that came then was Elizabeth Keckley, the mulatto woman who carried solace and ministering hands, and who was given trust and confidence that no others received.

Mary Clemmer Ames fathomed some of the bitterness of the hour. "Mrs. Lincoln bewept her husband. There is no doubt but that, in that black hour, she suffered great injustice. She loved her husband, with the intensity of a nature, deep and strong, within a narrow channel. The shock of his untimely taking-off, might have excused a woman of loftier nature than hers for any accompanying paralysis."

This was nearly the word, "paralysis." She lay physically helpless for days and wandered mentally and called for death to take her, crying she had lost all worth living for. It was five weeks before she was able to leave the White House. "It was not strange she stayed five weeks," wrote Mary Clemmer Ames. "It would have been stranger had she been able to have left it sooner. It was her misfortune that she had so armed public sympathy against her, by years of indifference to the sorrow of others, that when her own hour of supreme anguish came, there were few to comfort her, and many to assail. She had made many unpopular innovations upon the old serene and stately régime of the President's house. Never a reign of concord in her best day, in her hour of affliction it degenerated into absolute anarchy. The long-time steward [overseer and caretaker] had been dethroned, that Mrs. Lincoln might manage according to her own will. While she was shut in with her woe, the White House was left without a responsible protector. The rabble ranged through it at will. Silver and dining-ware were carried off, and have never been recovered. It was plundered, not only of ornaments, but of heavy articles of furniture. Costly sofas and chairs were cut and injured. Exquisite lace curtains were torn into rags, and carried off in pieces."

While all of this was going on downstairs, Mrs. Lincoln in her apartments upstairs refused to see any one but servants, while day after day immense boxes containing her personal effects were leaving the White House for the West. "The size and number of these boxes," noted Mrs. Ames, "with the fact of the pillaged aspect of the White House, led to the accusation, which so roused public feeling against her, that she was robbing the National House, and carrying the national property with her into retirement. This accusation, which clings to her to this day [1871], was probably unjust. Her personal effects, in all likeliness, amounted to as much as that of nearly all other Presidents' wives together, and the vandals who roamed at large through the length and breadth of the White House, were quite sufficient to account for all its missing treasures."

Broken Woman

THE TEN years between 1865 and 1875 were desperate for poor Mary Todd Lincoln. When the tongues of many begin wagging with a war-time hate there are reputations created, impressions spread, which are true only in the sense that the apparitions in concave or convex mirrors are in proportion. Mary Clemmer Ames in her book, "Ten Years in Washington," issued eight years after Mrs. Lincoln left the White House, recognized that the pictures of Mrs. Lincoln had run into riotous caricatures and wrote, "The public did Mrs. Lincoln injustice, in considering her an ignorant, illiterate woman. She was well born, gently reared, and her education above the average standard given to girls in her youth. She is a fair mistress of the French language, and in English can write a more graceful letter than one educated woman in fifty. She has quick perceptions, and an almost unrivalled power of mimicry. The only amusement of her desolate days, while shut in from the world in Chicago, when she refused to see her dearest friends and took comfort in the thought that she had been chosen as the object of preëminent affliction, was to repeat in tone, gesture, and expression, the words, looks and actions of men and women who, in the splendor of her life in Washington, had happened to offend her. Her lack was not a lack of keen faculties, or of fair culture, but a constitutional inability to rise to the action of high motive in a time when every true soul in the nation seemed to be impelled to unselfish deeds for its rescue. She was incapable of lofty, impersonal impulse. She was self-centered, and never in any experience rose above herself. According to circumstances, her own ambitions, her own pleasures, her own sufferings, made the sensation which absorbed and consumed every other. As a President's wife she could not rise above the level of her nature, and it was her misfortune that she never even approached the bound of her opportunity."

This is almost equivalent to saying that Mary Todd Lincoln never grew up, that she kept a child mind in the body of a matured woman, that she could not learn responsibility and meet it, that in her later years she had her mind fixed on the same shows and baubles of life that please a girl at a tea party for dolls. This would be too easy and offhand an explanation of the tumults that drove Mary Todd Lincoln through life. If she is to be compared with other Presidents' wives, other White House ladies whose performances rate higher in history for conduct and sacrifice, it may be she has an alibi, apology so perfect that her ghost could answer, "Did God in His infinite wisdom ever weigh down any

White House woman with a devastating curse such as rode in my blood and brain?"

There are crippled brains on which it is no more wise to visit impatience or excoriation or ordinary verdicts of guilty, than upon crippled bodies. We do not kick the physically clumsy for being what they are. Neither can we deal with the mentally thwarted in a vocabulary of blame. They are in a world outside the realm of sanity, balance, respectability, serenity, sweetness and light.

Letter after letter poured from her in which she cried life was too heavy for her, the burning too fierce. Part of it was the acting of a frustrated and furious woman trying to impose her will on a United States Congress which for years resisted her efforts towards a pension. Most of her crying out loud, publicly and privately, however, ran back to the pressure of tongs of fate that clamped tighter and tighter in the lobes of her brain. She was, as her physician and friend later declared, the victim of a cerebral disease. When she hurled petty and spiteful accusations in a way to lead few people or none to believe what she was saying, she was speaking with the tongue of an irresponsible woman. When she tried to dramatize herself as a pauper, "seeking lodging from one place to another" it was the impulse of a disordered brain. When the administrator of her husband's estate made the public record, as required by law, that the property for equal sharing among Abraham Lincoln's three heirs was valued at $110,000.00, her mind was so far gone that she could not realize it was time for her to drop the rôle of a woman wronged in money matters. During many years of her life she had overridden obstacles, she had exercised a stubborn and commanding power that brought her things she wanted. The old Covenanter blood ran deep in her; she was a fighter; and she would fight on now against simple circumstances impossible to surmount. Her waning mind could no longer grasp obstacles in the face of which an intelligent woman would know her cue was complete silence.

She still had vitality, sometimes furious in its rush at her enemies, and again frantic and futile, lacking direction, not knowing how or when to hit. It may even be that the pathos of her fate was known to her. She may have suspected that her mind and temperament were too imperfect for adjustment to the human equation into which life had thrust her. And what flickers of suspicion she had were overcome by her pride, by her abiding belief that destiny had set her for a Great Lady and she would enact that rôle to the last breath of her combative spirit. Yet it seems also that even though she did believe she could surmount this or that barrier, that she could win in this or that contest against individuals, there was nevertheless a whole of life—a vast brutal phantasmagoria—which had her conquered in middle age and in her youth. She was writing in 1865 that "life is indeed a heavy burden and I do not care how soon I am called hence." Also: "My heart is indeed broken, and without my beloved husband, I do not care to live."

When her letters printed in the New York *World* announced a public auction of her personal wardrobe for the purpose of getting funds for herself and family to live on, she had rushed into it on an impulse with no forethought as to the misery such an action would give to the few who were loyal to her for what she had been in the past. She sent a letter to Elizabeth Keckley. "I am writing this morning with a broken heart after a sleepless night of great mental suffering. R. [Robert] came up last evening like a maniac, and almost threatening his life, looking like death, because the letters of the *World* were published in yesterday's [Chicago] papers. I could not refrain from weeping when I saw him so miserable. But yet, my dear good Lizzie, was it not to protect myself and help others—and was not my motive and action of the purest kind? Pray for me that this cup of affliction may pass from me, or be sanctified to me. I weep whilst I am writing." She ended the letter: "I am nearly losing my reason."

She could fight the outside world and fling back spite for spite but the wild reproaches of her eldest son, "looking like death," gave her a night of tears. Robert, just two years out of Harvard and looking forward to a career as a lawyer, with his inclinations and prospects associated with the respectable and wealthy classes, had been shocked at the sudden news that his mother was publicly selling to the highest bidder one lace dress, one flounced dress, five lace shawls, three camel-hair shawls, one lace parasol cover, one sable boa, one white boa, one set of furs, two Paisley shawls, two gold bracelets, sixteen dresses, two opera cloaks, one feather cape, one diamond ring, one child's shawl, twenty-eight yards of silk, and other articles. From the way Robert behaved his mother knew that he and others were ashamed of her and afraid of what she would do next. The "old clothes speculation," as her sale was designated, was the farthest she had ever drifted from being in public a Great Lady. Before her time more than one First Lady of the Land had been accused of taking away White House belongings. Yet

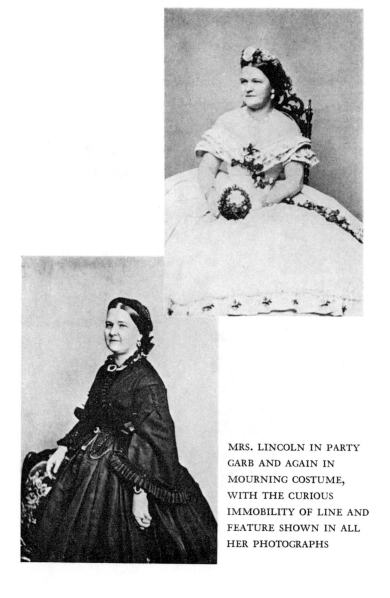

MRS. LINCOLN IN PARTY
GARB AND AGAIN IN
MOURNING COSTUME,
WITH THE CURIOUS
IMMOBILITY OF LINE AND
FEATURE SHOWN IN ALL
HER PHOTOGRAPHS

THE IRREPRES-
SIBLE TAD

A LATER LIKE-
NESS OF TAD

Taken in Frank-
furt, Germany

MRS. LINCOLN IN DARK ATTIRE

(Photographs from the collection of Oliver R. Barrett)

none of the mistresses of the Executive Mansion had ever invited the public to an auction of her personal apparel, jewels, keepsakes.

After a night of tears Mary Lincoln wrote, "I pray for death this morning. Only my darling Taddie prevents my taking my life. I shall have to endure a round of abuse from the Republicans because I dared to relieve a few of my wants." And it came to her that her face, her looks, were changing for the worse, and she wrote, "What a world of anguish this is—and how I have been made to suffer! You would not recognize me now. The glass shows me a pale, wretched, haggard face, and my dresses are like bags on me." She was becoming more of a stranger, an alien to some who had known her for years. Robert was writing to a young woman he was to marry soon, "I have no doubt that a great many good and amiable people wonder why I do not take charge of her affairs and keep them straight but it is very hard to deal with one who is sane on all subjects but one. You would hardly believe it possible, but my mother protests to me that she is in actual want and nothing I can do or say will convince her to the contrary. Do you see that I am likely to have a good deal of trouble in the future, do what I can to prevent it."

The troubled woman wrote of "debts staring me in

the face," of lacking "the simplest daily necessities," of pressing unpaid bills. "I wish I could forget myself." She recalled her "angel boy in Heaven"—Willie Lincoln whose death in 1862 had been a shock to her. "He was too pure for Earth and God recalled His own."

She mentioned suffering with "fearful" headaches. She wrote of "friends," of "false-hearted villains" trying to ruin her. "The agitation of mind has very much impaired my health." She apologized for an explosion of behavior. "Never, dear Lizzie think of my great nervousness the night before we parted; I had been so harassed with my fears." She went deep in pity for herself: "If I had committed murder in every city in this blessed Union, I could not be more traduced." She wrote in October, 1867, "A piece in the morning *Tribune,* signed 'B,' pretending to be a lady, says there is no doubt Mrs. L. *is* deranged—has been for years past and will end her years in a lunatic asylum. They would doubtless like me to begin it *now."* She wrote the same month, "The Springfield *Journal* had an editorial a few days since, with the important information that Mrs. Lincoln had been known to be *deranged* for years, and should be pitied for all her *strange acts."* Her immediate thought in that connection was that "in the comfortable stealings by contracts from the Government, these low creatures are allowed to hurl their malicious wrath at me, with no one to defend me or protect me, if I should starve." And while she wrote and spoke of starving, of economy, of being clothed shabbily, Judge David Davis filed a statement of the assets of the estate of her husband, amounting to $110,000.00.

The impression was definite now in many circles that Mary Todd Lincoln was mentally unsound, was a pathological case requiring attention, treatment, at least retirement from affairs which would bring her in any way before the public. She met these requirements for a time by going to London and continental Europe, taking Tad with her. They lived quietly. Tad studied with a tutor who came daily in London. His mother was anxious about his education. They went together among wonderful mountains and valleys. She read French novels. She saw few of her homeland people. She wrote one letter reporting foggy weather and rain, rain, rain, beating on the window. "The loneliness of this winter words could not express, nor pen write its horrors."

She wrote long letters to Mary Harlan Lincoln, who had married Robert. Some of these were brimming with vitality and affection. She was better for living in strange lands and among strangers. So it seemed at moments. Yet the old headaches still visited her; she told of attacks of neuralgia in the head. It almost seemed she knew the storms of life were over for her, that her strength was gone for any more of the bitter contests into which she had flung herself. "I am well aware without my physician so frequently repeating to me—that quiet is necessary for my life."

Now she had fairly well stepped out of the public gaze. The reports and rumors of her in the public prints had nearly died down. They flared up, however, in connection with the bill of Senator Charles Sumner to award her a pension of $5,000 a year, the amount of interest due her on her husband's salary if he had lived to serve out his term. In the end the bill passed with the pension fixed at $3,000 a year. While the bill was under consideration Mrs. Lincoln heard of the sister of a United States congressman being in Paris. And she wrote an eight-page letter on black-bordered paper, pleas and arguments for her pension, asking help of the congressman's sister. The letter was "confidential." She wished it burned. She made personal allusions to the wife of President Grant, to the wife of E. B. Washburne, French ambassador. These personal allusions were uncalled for. Once more the public prints in America dealt with her griefs and ways.

There could be little doubt hot wires were being drawn through her eyes. There were steel springs in her head. The tongs of an iron fate pressed between her aching temples.

She went home—to America—to Chicago. Tad Lincoln, now eighteen years old, a whimsical and promising boy, was stricken with typhoid and died. And no one could say of the mother and widow mourning at the grave of the third of her four sons that her life had been laid in pleasant paths.

She made mistakes and was blamed. A friend inquired why she was blamed with "her brain on fire with pain."

Bitter Cups

Is EACH of our lives a book? And when it is done and over, having a first and last chapter, can we turn the pages backward or forward and read what the years did to this or that one of us? Perhaps this is so and we can turn to the year 1875 and see what happened to Mary Todd Lincoln.

She had left Chicago where her one living son Robert had married and begun law practice. And from Florida where she was spending the winter she suddenly sent a telegram in March to Dr. Ralph N. Isham, their family physician. The life of her boy was in danger; she called on the doctor to save her boy. She was taking a train for Chicago.

When she arrived in Chicago her boy, in very good health, and Dr. Isham met her at the railroad depot. And talking with her boy and seeing his face smoothed out her fears and she seemed to be a sensible and lively woman again.

The long trip from Florida had been nice and pleasant, she told them—except that in Jacksonville, where she bought a cup of coffee, some enemy had put poison in the coffee; she refused to drink the coffee believing it would mean her death. Thus there were people lying in wait seeking her death. So her talk implied.

Would she go with her son to his home and stay?

No, she couldn't, she must go to the Grand Pacific Hotel, in the center of the turmoil of Chicago. And the son must go with her to the hotel and stay with her.

So that night and following nights Robert Lincoln slept in a room next to his mother—though his sleep was interrupted. His mother would knock on the door of his room calling that she was in danger. To ease her mind he slept on a lounge in her room. Or again she came into his room and he gave her his bed while he took a couch.

She screamed, "You are going to murder me," when Robert intercepted her in a downgoing elevator. A fire would destroy Chicago and Robert's house would be the only one left standing, she told him. She brought forth from a pocket and showed to Robert $57,000 worth of stocks and bonds she was carrying on her person. She told him that a man had taken her pocketbook, promising to return it at a certain hour; the man was a Wandering Jew she had met in Florida; she seated herself next to a wall and pretended to be repeating what the man was saying to her through the wall.

The joy she had shown at first on her return from Florida passed away. She spoke of physical torments inflicted on her. Needles of flame were being drawn through her head. A watch must be kept for persons hiding near by waiting to murder her. An Indian was pulling wires out of her eyes. There were steel springs in her head which doctors were taking out.

In two days shopping in April she bought $772.03 worth of sashes, ribbons, ties, pointe lace, silk handkerchiefs, gloves, hose, pointe collars. She bought two Shetland *coiffures,* two parasols, three dozen handkerchiefs, seventeen pairs of gloves. She bought three watches for $450, jewelry costing $700, a bolt of silk, $200 worth of soaps and perfumes. Though having no house of her own and refusing to live at her son's house, she bought lace curtains, $213.00 worth at Ellen & Mackey, $336.83 worth at Hollister & Phelps.

Naturally by now there was town talk about her. The chambermaids and bellboys at the hotel said nothing they could do pleased her. The hotel manager was worrying and suggested some other place would make a better residence for her.

On May 18, 1874, Dr. Ralph N. Isham dated a document of that day and wrote:

"I hereby certify that I have examined Mrs. Mary Lincoln—widow—and that I am of the opinion that she is insane and a fit subject for hospital treatment."

On the next day attorneys for Robert T. Lincoin
(Ayer & Koles, and Leonard Swett) entered in the
county court of Cook County, before Judge M. R. M.
Wallace an application to try the question of sanity. It
read to begin with: "The petition of Robert T. Lincoln
would respectfully represent that his mother, Mary
Lincoln, widow of Abraham Lincoln, deceased, a resident of Cook County is insane, and that it would be
for her benefit and for the safety of the community
that she should be confined." It named seventeen witnesses who should be summoned, estimated her estate
to be valued not exceeding $75,000.00 and prayed for a
conservator to be appointed to manage and control her
estate.

On the same day the county court clerk signed a
writ to the sheriff stating in part: "You are therefore
hereby commanded to arrest said Mary Lincoln, widow
of Abraham Lincoln, deceased, to have her on the 19th
day of May, A. D. 1875, at 2 o'clock P. M. before our
County Court, and then and there to await and abide
the result of the trial."

On the same day of May 19th a jury of twelve men
heard the witnesses and brought a verdict, "We . . .
are satisfied that the said Mary Lincoln is insane and
is a fit person to be sent to a State Hospital." Her age

was fifty-six years, it was set forth. "The disease is of unknown duration; the cause is unknown."

Besides retail storekeepers, and the son Robert, five physicians testified. Dr. Willis Danforth said he had treated Mrs. Lincoln several weeks in 1873 for fever and nervous derangement of the head. She had imaginings that "some one was at work on her head, an Indian was removing the bones from her face and pulling wires out of her eyes." He visited her again in 1874 when she was suffering from nervous debility. "She complained that some one was taking steel springs from her head and would not let her rest. She was going to die within a few days, had been admonished to that effect by her husband. She imagined that she heard raps on a table conveying the time of her death, and would sit and ask questions and repeat the supposed answer the table would give." On general topics her conversation was rational. Her derangement did not arise from bodily condition nor physical disease. "I . . . am of the opinion that she is insane."

Robert T. Lincoln closed his difficult session as a witness with saying, "I have had a conference with her cousin and Major Stuart of Springfield, and Judge Davis of the Supreme Court, all of whom advised me in the course I have taken. I do not regard it safe to

Office of Dr. RALPH N. ISHAM,

47 South Clark Street,

OFFICE HOURS:
From 11 A.M. to 1 P.M.
RESIDENCE,
321 NORTH DEARBORN ST.,
(WASHINGTON SQUARE)

Chicago, May 18th 1875.

I hereby certify that I have examined Mrs Mary Lincoln — widow — and that I am of the opinion that she is insane and a fit subject for Hospital treatment

Ralph N. Isham M.D.

THE CERTIFICATE OF MRS. LINCOLN'S PHYSICIAN ON HER MENTAL CONDITION

To the Hon. M. R. M. WALLACE, Judge of said Court:

The petition of ...Robert T. Lincoln...

would respectfully represent that ...Mrs. mother, Mary Lincoln, widow of Abraham Lincoln deced... a resident of Cook County is insane, and that it would be for ...her... benefit and for the safety of the community that ...she... should be confined in the Cook County Hospital or the Illinois State Hospital for the insane. The facts in ...her... case can be proven by...Ralph N. Isham...

a regular practicing physician, and by ...Willis Danforth, Samuel M. Turner, Mary Gavin, E. E. Stone, C. J. Dalrymple, S. L. Leopold, Mahala Clark, Maggie Gavin, C. J. Dalrymple, jr., Frank M. Turner, John Fitzhenry, J. S. Smith, Charles S. Smith, and Edwin A. Brown and others who reside in this City ... all whom are residents of this County, and that the said ...Mary Lincoln...

has property and effects consisting of ...Negotiable securities... and ...other personal property...

the value of which does not exceed the sum of ...Seventy-five thousand... Dollars.

THE PETITION OF ROBERT LINCOLN TO THE COUNTY COURT OF COOK COUNTY allow her to remain longer unrestrained. She has long been a source of great anxiety. . . . She has no home, and does not visit my house because of a misunderstanding with my wife. She has always been kind to me. She has been of unsound mind since the death of her husband, and has been irresponsible for the last ten years. I regard her as eccentric and unmanageable. There was no cause for her recent purchases, as her trunks are filled with dresses she never wears. She never wears jewelry."

The hearing was conducted quietly, decently. The jurors were business and professional men chosen to do a difficult and responsible task of citizenship with delicacy and honor. On June 14th Robert T. Lincoln was issued letters of conservatorship by the county court, "duly appointed Conservator for Mary Lincoln, widow of Abraham Lincoln, diseased." The usual form was observed by the county court and a statement of the trial and its results, with the names of the jurors, was entered on a large sheet titled "Lunatic Record. County Court of Cook County." The Court Clerk, H. Lieb, filed papers marked "Mary Lincoln, Lunatic."

It was a heavy day's work, done by men with heavy hearts. The color of death was in the air. The proceedings had a touch of burial service in them. Something

148

and our last resort — a plain yet genteel boarding, does not exempt, us, from charges, that I shall have to exert myself, in the future, to meet — I will write no more to day, for I became so thoroughly chilled on yesterday, that my limbs — ache with pain and I am sure, the terrible trial we are passing through — will only pain your gentle heart, by the recapitulation —

With much love, I remain always truly

Mary Lincoln.

MARY LINCOLN WRITES MRS. J. H. ORNE
JAN. 4, 1866
(In the collection of Oliver R. Barrett)

ROBERT TODD LINCOLN
IN MANHOOD

ROBERT TODD LINCOLN
IN YOUTH AS A
HARVARD GRADUATE

(Both in the collection
of Oliver R. Barrett)

that had been alive, with control and direction, was gone. Something that once had vitality and bloom had become victim to rot and dissolution while yet partly alive. Death itself with the complete paralysis of the mind and the laying away of the cold remains of the physical structure in the ground—this is easy to gaze on as compared with looking from day to day and month to month at a mind in ruins, being eaten away by a slow destroyer. The test of living next to this personal tragedy came hard on Robert T. Lincoln. For fifty years after it he was a shy man. His shyness was spoken of. It could be traced back to any one of several tragedies to which his eyes and ears were witness.

Mary Lincoln was taken now to Batavia, Illinois, a place set on hills overlooking long slopes of the Fox River Valley. In a private sanitarium under the care of a distinguished specialist she was better off than she had been for years. Robert T. Lincoln wrote a letter to Mrs. J. H. Orne, a long-time friend of his mother and himself. "Six physicians informed me that by longer delay I was making myself morally responsible for some very probable tragedy, which might occur at any moment. Some of my Eastern friends have criticized the public proceedings in court, which seemed to them unnecessary. Against this there was no help, for we have a statute in this State which imposes a very heavy penalty on any one depriving an insane person of his liberty without the verdict of a jury. My mother is, I think, under as good care and as happily situated as is possible under the circumstances. She is in the private part of the house of Dr. Patterson and her associates are the members of his family only. With them she walks and drives whenever she likes and takes her meals with them or in her own room as she chooses, and she tells me she likes them all very much. The [her] expression of surprise at my action which was telegraphed East, and which you doubtless saw, was the first and last expression of the kind she has uttered and we are on the best of terms. Indeed my consolation in this sad affair is in thinking that she herself is happier in every way, than she has been in ten years. So far as I can see she does not realize her situation at all. I can tell you nothing as to the probability of her restoration. It must be the work of some time if it occurs."

It was a letter more like his father than any we know of that ever came from Robert T. Lincoln. He ended it: "The responsibility that has been and is now on me is one that I would gladly share if it was possible to do so, but being alone as I am, I can only do my duty as it is given me to see it."

State of Illinois,

COUNTY OF COOK. } ss.

In the County Court of Cook County:

THE PEOPLE OF THE STATE OF ILLINOIS,

To the Sheriff of said County:—GREETING:

Whereas, it has been represented to the Honorable M. R. M. WALLACE, Judge of this Court, by _Robert T. Lincoln_ in a petition duly verified, that _Mary Lincoln widow of Abraham Lincoln deceased_ is believed to be insane, and whereas said Judge has appointed the hearing of said petition for the _nineteenth_ day of _May_ A. D. 1875 at 2 o'clock P.M.

After three months in the Batavia sanitarium Mary
Lincoln was taken for a visit with her sister Elizabeth
(Mrs. Ninian W. Edwards) in Springfield, Illinois.
From September 13, 1875, to June 7, 1876, Robert T.
Lincoln paid checks to Ninian W. Edwards ranging
from $100 to $875. The total of $4,599.28 was itemized
in the report of the conservator to the Cook County
court as being "for expenses of Mrs. Lincoln during her
visit and sojourn at Springfield, Illinois, being money
sent Hon. N. W. Edwards, and by him given to Mrs.
Lincoln, to be expended by her for her comfort and
support." Every service and attention advised by skilled
physicians, besides anything of help that money could
buy, was hers. Her sister Elizabeth, whom she called
"Lizzie," was a cheerful presence, was thoughtful. So
Mary Lincoln grew better.

Her jewels had been taken away from her. And she
wanted them. Also there were nine trunks of dresses
and other personal belongings of old days which she
wanted. And on December 15, 1875, Robert T. Lincoln
appeared before Judge Wallace of the Cook County
court and set forth that "Mrs. Lincoln is exceedingly
anxious and desirous to have the custody and use of the
articles of personal jewelry contained in a Tin Box
mentioned by the undersigned in the inventory filed

You are therefore hereby commanded to arrest said *Mary Lincoln*

Widow of *Abraham Lincoln deceased* to have her on the 19th

day of *May* ..... A.D. 1875 at 2 o'clock P.M., before our County

Court, and then and there to await and abide the result of the trial.

And have you then and there this Writ, and make due service as the law directs.

Witness, HERMANN LIEB, Clerk of our said Court, and

the Seal of said Court at Chicago, in said County, this 19th

A.D. 1875

day of *May*

Hermann Lieb

Clerk.

LOWER HALF OF THE WARRANT FOR THE ARREST OF MARY LINCOLN

by him. The Box is now in the Fidelity Safe Depository for safe keeping and Mrs. Lincoln has its key." Judge David Davis and Leonard Swett had been consulted as friends, "familiar with the facts of Mrs. Lincoln's case" and they advised compliance with her request; she ought to be allowed her jewels and gowns of old days if she wanted them. The conservator "does not think Mrs. Lincoln will make any improper disposition of the articles contained in the box"; possession would benefit her. So she regained her jewels. Also, three days later the court gave leave for her to again have nine trunks "containing wearing apparel principally," the conservator believed. "She needs for her use a great part thereof."

When Mary Lincoln had been one year and nearly a month in classification and under treatment as insane, her attorney, Isaac Arnold, petitioned the Cook County Court for removal of her conservator and a restoration of all rights, privileges, and property. On June 15 a sworn statement of Ninian W. Edwards was filed with the court testifying, "Mrs. Lincoln has been with me for nine or ten months, and her friends all think she is a proper person to take charge of her own affairs." The statement thus opened and then went on to repeat, "She has been with me about nine months,

② Personal Property of which the value is not estimated.

A tin box containing personal Jewelry, and also nine trunks containing wearing apparel and other articles, in name of Kimmie.

All stored for Safe Keeping in the "Fidelity-Safety-Depository" in Chicago, having been locked and the Keys retained by Mrs. Lincoln. (both value) $5000.00

Summary.

Cash .... $ 1,029.35
United States Bonds and Stocks 58,000.00
Personal Bond 8,895.00
Personal property of which value is given 5,542.83
                                       Total $73,467.18

and her friends all of them recognize that she is a fit person to take care of and manage her own affairs. That she is in such condition that she can manage her own affairs." One circumstance was detailed: "She has not spent all that she was allowed to spend during the past year, and we all think she is in a condition to take charge of her own affairs."

And on the same day of June 15, 1876, the court removed the conservator, Robert T. Lincoln, restored Mary Lincoln to her rights and property, and she received from Robert T. Lincoln an elaborate, scrupulous and thoroughly detailed accounting of her money, estate, pension papers, bonds, leases, expenses for physicians, attendants, nurses, railroad fare, telegrams, storage and express charges, including $6.00 for repair of a music box and $151.00 for hack hire and shadowing by Pinkerton detectives.

And now as a free woman again, free to come and go, free to make her own decisions, what would Mary Todd Lincoln do? She told her sister she couldn't stand it to meet old friends. "Lizzie, they will never cease to regard me a lunatic, I feel it in their soothing manner. If I should say the moon is made of green cheese they would heartily and smilingly agree with me. I love you, but I cannot stay. I would be much less unhappy in the midst of strangers." And to strangers she went. She put the Atlantic Ocean between herself and her old friends. In Germany, France, Italy, she lived—mostly alone, often without servant or companion, and sometimes with no letters passing between her and Robert so that for periods of time he did not know where she was—a worn struggler having only memories to live with— letting it be known as little as possible who she was— hiding her name as a fugitive. She wrote few letters. One told of her pleasure at being far from "the border ruffian west."

She was in her sixtieth year in Pau, France, in December of 1879, living cheaply, doing without a servant. And mounting a stepladder one day to fix a picture over a mantelpiece, she fell to the floor. She was kept to her bed with inflammation of the spinal cord and a partial crippling of the legs. She got up and managed to travel to Nice where again she had to go to bed for rest. She improved enough to board a ship for the homeland. Something told her it was time now to go home.

Aboard the ship was the world-famous actress Madam Sarah Bernhardt. Arriving at the Port of New York a crowd of people and a group of newspaper reporters were at the dock—and there were cheers and excitement—over the arrival of Bernhardt. The New York *Sun* told of how it was necessary for a policeman to put his hand on the shoulder of a little old woman with a wrinkling face and streaks of white in her hair; she must stand back while a path was made for the footlight queen to her carriage.

Mary Lincoln stayed a little time in New York for consultation and medical treatment. Then Springfield, Illinois, again—home with sister Lizzie. There she hid herself as best she could; weather permitting, the windows were shut and the shades pulled down. Her talk among the few friends who saw her was of her husband, of her poverty, of ingratitude and misunderstanding. It was a brief interlude of joy when her son, Robert, and his wife arrived and set in her lap their girl child named Mary for her grandmother.

More and more she shrank from the outside world. When invited for a drive she might or might not go. If she did the carriage curtains must be drawn. She was weary of faces. In earlier years she wanted everybody, the whole world, to see her. That was past. Now she wanted to be alone with what was so deeply past. She wrote in a letter, "Ah, my dear friend, you will rejoice when you know that I have gone to my husband and children."

She lingered on, muttering of shadows that waited for her beyond this world. She sought healing in a trip to New York in March of 1882. In Springfield again she sat at the fireside of the Edwards home with a few friends. Summer came, she weakened, lay abed many days racked with boils. She took off her wedding ring from a swollen finger. One Friday in July she walked across the room without help. But she wasn't getting better. For the next day she could neither walk nor talk nor eat. Paralysis crept up into her body.

In the room where she had sat so much with candle-light and shadow, the evening of all her years came a little after sunset on July 16, 1882. This was in the same house where nearly forty years earlier she was married. They carried a burial casket out over the threshold her feet touched as a bride—and that was all.

A newspaper had mentioned her wedding ring as taken off. "It is of Etruscan gold and is now quite thin from wear. It is inscribed with 'A. L. to Mary, Nov. 4, 1842. Love is Eternal.' The ring will be put on and probably be buried with her."

Index

161

INDEX